Reptiles and Amphibians

John Stidworthy

WITH CONTRIBUTIONS BY

Jill Bailey

Facts On File

New York • Oxford

REPTILES AND AMPHIBIANS
The Encyclopedia of the Animal World

Managing Editor: Lionel Bender
Art Editor: Ben White
Text Editor: Barbara Taylor-Cork
Assistant Editor: Madeleine Samuel
Project Editor: Graham Bateman
Production: Clive Sparling, Joanna
   Turner

Media conversion and typesetting:
   Robert and Peter MacDonald,
   Una Macnamara

AN EQUINOX BOOK

Planned and produced by:
Equinox (Oxford) Limited,
Musterlin House, Jordan Hill Road,
Oxford OX2 8DP, England

Prepared by Lionheart Books

Library of Congress
Cataloging-in-Publication Data
Stidworthy, John, 1943-
Reptiles and amphibians/John Stidworthy
with contributions by Jill Bailey.
p.   cm. —— (The Encyclopedia of the
   animal world)
Includes index.
Summary: Provides brief descriptions of
various amphibians and reptiles.

1. Reptiles – Juvenile literature. 2.
Amphibians – Juvenile literature. [1.
Amphibians. 2. Reptiles.]   I. Bailey, Jill. II.
Title. III. Series.

QL644.2.S75 1989   597.6 - dc19
88-33317 CIP AC

ISBN 0-8160-1965-7

Published in North America by
Facts On File, Inc.,
460 Park Avenue South,
New York, N.Y. 10016

Origination by Alpha Reprographics Ltd,
Perivale, Middx, England

Printed in Italy.

10 9 8 7 6 5 4 3 2 1

FACT PANEL: Key to symbols denoting general features of animals

SYMBOLS WITH NO WORDS

Activity time

- ● Nocturnal
- ◓ Daytime
- ◖ Dawn/Dusk
- ○ All the time

Group size

- ◪ Solitary
- ▦ Pairs
- ◾ Small groups (up to 10)
- ■ Large groups
- ◪ Variable

Conservation status

- ☠ All species threatened
- ⚕ Some species threatened
- No species threatened (no symbol)

SYMBOLS NEXT TO HEADINGS

Habitat

- ◣ General
- ◢ Mountain/Moorland
- ◢ Desert
- 〰 Sea
- ■ Amphibious

- ◿ Tundra
- ◢ Forest/Woodland
- ● Grassland
- ⊗ Freshwater

Diet

- ■ Other animals
- ■ Plants
- ◪ Animals and Plants

Breeding

- ◎ Seasonal (at fixed times)
- ◔ Non-seasonal (at any time)

CONTENTS

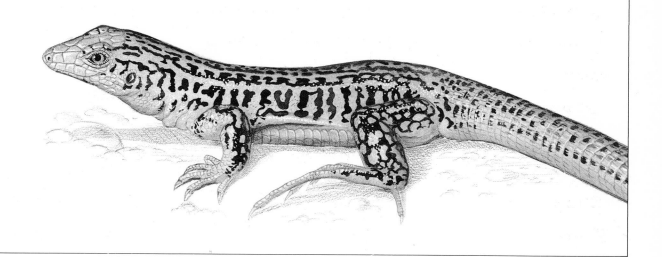

PREFACE

The National Wildlife Federation

For the wildlife of the world, 1936 was a very big year. That's when the National Wildlife Federation formed to help conserve the millions of species of animals and plants that call Earth their home. In trying to do such an important job, the Federation has grown to be the largest conservation group of its kind.

Today, plants and animals face more dangers than ever before. As the human population grows and takes over more and more land, the wild places of the world disappear. As people produce more and more chemicals and cars and other products to make life better for themselves, the environment often becomes worse for wildlife.

But there is some good news. Many animals are better off today than when the National Wildlife Federation began. Alligators, wild turkeys, deer, wood ducks, and others are thriving – thanks to the hard work of everyone who cares about wildlife.

The Federation's number one job has always been education. We teach kids the wonders of nature through *Your Big Backyard* and *Ranger Rick* magazines and our annual National Wildlife Week celebration. We teach grown-ups the importance of a clean environment through *National Wildlife* and *International Wildlife* magazines. And we help teachers teach about wildlife with our environmental education activity series called *Naturescope*.

The National Wildlife Federation is nearly five million people, all working as one. We all know that by helping wildlife, we are also helping ourselves. Together we have helped pass laws that have cleaned up our air and water, protected endangered species, and left grand old forests standing tall.

You can help too. Every time you plant a bush that becomes a home to a butterfly, every time you help clean a lake or river of trash, every time you walk instead of asking for a ride in a car – you are part of the wildlife team.

You are also doing your part by learning all you can about the wildlife of the world. That's why the National Wildlife Federation is happy to help bring you this Encyclopedia. We hope you enjoy it.

Jay D. Hair, President
National Wildlife Federation

INTRODUCTION

The Encyclopedia of the Animal World surveys the main groups and species of animals alive today. Written by a team of specialists, it includes the most current information and the newest ideas on animal behavior and survival. The Encyclopedia looks at how the shape and form of an animal reflect its life-style – the ways in which a creature's size, color, feeding methods and defenses have all evolved in relationship to a particular diet, climate and habitat. Discussed also are the ways in which human activities often disrupt natural ecosystems and threaten the survival of many species.

In this Encyclopedia the animals are grouped on the basis of their body structure and their evolution from common ancestors. Thus, there are single volumes or groups of volumes on mammals, birds, reptiles and amphibians, fish, insects and so on. Within these major categories, the animals are grouped according to their feeding habits or general life-styles. Because there is so much information on the animals in two of these major categories, there are four volumes devoted to mammals (The Small Plant-Eaters; The Hunters; The Large Plant-Eaters; Primates, Insect-Eaters and Baleen Whales) and three to birds (The Waterbirds; The Aerial Hunters; The Plant- and Seed-Eaters).

This volume, Reptiles and Amphibians, includes entries on salamanders, newts, toads, frogs, turtles, tortoises, lizards, snakes, alligators and crocodiles. Together they number some 10,400 species. The amphibians represent the group of animals that made the transition from the totally aquatic life of fishes and evolved the ability to move about freely on land yet need the water to breed. Reptiles took the conquest of the land a stage further and became completely independent from water.

Both amphibians and reptiles are "cold-blooded" – their body temperature depends on the temperature of their surroundings – and, at least as adults, they all breathe with lungs rather than with gills as fish do. But these two groups of animals do have marked differences. Amphibians – the frogs, toads, salamanders, newts, mudpuppies and caecilians – have a soft, smooth skin that is permeable to water; reptiles are covered in coarse, dry scales that are impervious to water. The eggs of amphibians lack a waterproof outer covering and are always laid in water or in damp places, whereas the reptilian egg has a thick parchment-like or hard shell that holds moisture in, enabling the young to develop within it even on dry land.

Amphibians and reptiles are highly successful animals, as much so as mammals and birds, but they go about things in different ways. They are, for example, more efficient in their use of energy and, because of various special features that they possess, are able to live in environments that are inaccessible to other species. Most notably, reptiles can thrive in the driest of deserts.

Each article in this Encyclopedia is devoted to an individual species or group of closely related species. The text starts with a short scene-setting story that highlights one or more of the animal's unique features. It then continues with details of the most interesting aspects of the animal's physical features and abilities, diet and feeding behavior, and general life-style. It also covers conservation and the animal's relationships with people.

A fact panel provides easy reference to the main features of distribution (natural, not introductions to other areas by humans), habitat, diet, size, color and breeding. (An explanation of the color-coded symbols is given on page 2 of the book.) The panel also includes a list of the common and scientific (Latin) names of species mentioned in the main text and photo captions. For species illustrated in major artwork panels but not described elsewhere, the names are given in the caption accompanying the artwork. In such illustrations, all animals are shown to scale; actual dimensions may be found in the text. To help the reader appreciate the size of the animals, in the upper right part of the page at the beginning of an article are scale drawings comparing the size of the species with that of a human being (or of a human foot).

Many species of animal are threatened with extinction as a result of human activities. In this Encyclopedia the following terms are used to show the status of a species as defined by the International Union for the Conservation of Nature and Natural Resources:

Endangered – in danger of extinction unless their habitat is no longer destroyed and they are not hunted by people.

Vulnerable – likely to become endangered in the near future.

Rare – exist in small numbers but neither endangered nor vulnerable at present.

A glossary provides definitions of technical terms used in the book. A common name and scientific (Latin) name index provide easy access to text and illustrations.

WHAT IS AN AMPHIBIAN?

Most amphibians spend part of their lives in water and the rest of the time on land. The name amphibian comes from a combination of two Greek words, *amphi* and *bios*, meaning a double life. They include frogs, toads, newts and salamanders. Most have fish-like young called tadpoles.

Amphibians are vertebrates – they have a bony internal skeleton built around a backbone – the vertebral column. They are also "cold-blooded" or more correctly ectothermic; their body temperature depends upon the temperature of their surroundings. They are not able to produce their own body heat, and so cannot easily control the speed with which their body systems work. In cold weather, amphibians become cold and lazy, but in warm weather they are warm and very active. If their surroundings become too hot, they must retreat into the shade to cool down.

The skin of most amphibians is usually soft and moist. Some species have claw-like scales on the fingers and toes. Glands in an amphibian's skin produce a slimy mucus to keep the skin moist. The skin is not water-proof, so amphibians are generally found in moist places, which helps prevent their bodies drying out.

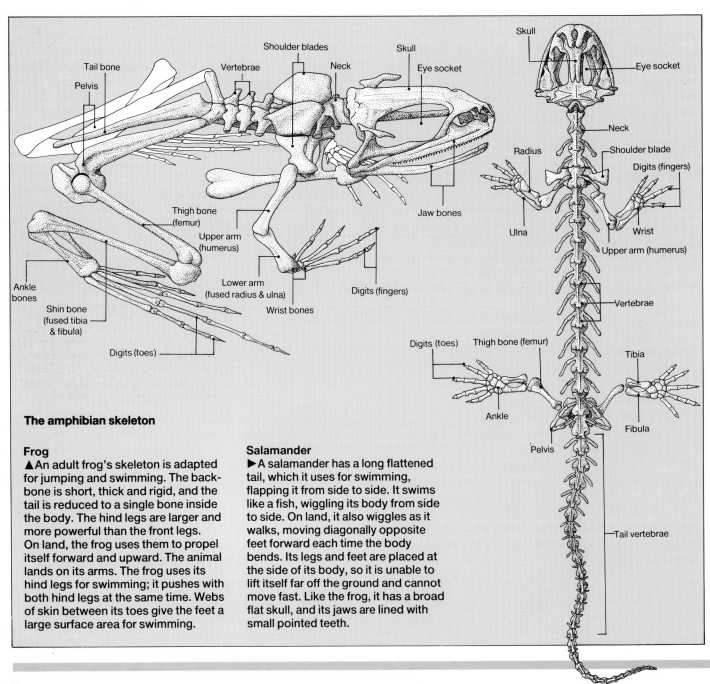

The amphibian skeleton

Frog
▲An adult frog's skeleton is adapted for jumping and swimming. The back-bone is short, thick and rigid, and the tail is reduced to a single bone inside the body. The hind legs are larger and more powerful than the front legs. On land, the frog uses them to propel itself forward and upward. The animal lands on its arms. The frog uses its hind legs for swimming; it pushes with both hind legs at the same time. Webs of skin between its toes give the feet a large surface area for swimming.

Salamander
▶A salamander has a long flattened tail, which it uses for swimming, flapping it from side to side. It swims like a fish, wiggling its body from side to side. On land, it also wiggles as it walks, moving diagonally opposite feet forward each time the body bends. Its legs and feet are placed at the side of its body, so it is unable to lift itself far off the ground and cannot move fast. Like the frog, it has a broad flat skull, and its jaws are lined with small pointed teeth.

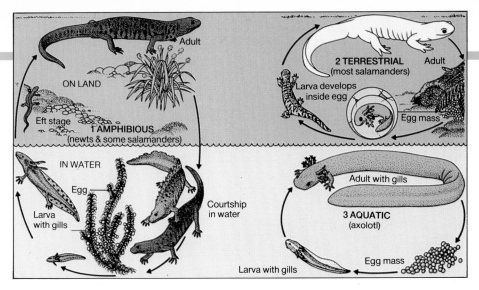

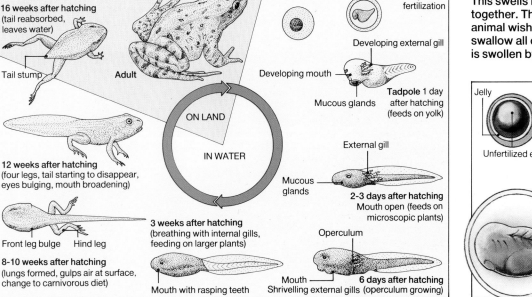

▲All salamanders and newts produce fish-like larvae that breathe using feathery external gills. Many are truly amphibious: the adults return to water to breed, and the larvae live and feed in the water until they develop lungs and are ready to live on land. Some spend their whole lives on land. The larvae of these species develop inside the egg until they can breathe air. The axolotl spends all its life in water. The adult is like a giant larva: it still has external gills.

▼Most frogs return to water to mate and lay their eggs. The fish-like tadpoles develop in the water. They crawl out on to land when their lungs are fully formed and their mouths are ready to start eating insects.

A DOUBLE LIFE

Young amphibians do not resemble their parents. They are called larvae. As they develop, they undergo a dramatic change in body shape, diet and life-style. This change is called metamorphosis, which means change of shape. Many amphibians return to water to breed, sometimes traveling several miles overland to reach their favorite breeding ponds. Those species that live in hot moist climates may breed at any time of the year. In tropical regions with a distinct wet and dry season, breeding often takes place as the rains begin. In temperate regions, breeding is usually in spring.

Male frogs and toads attract the females by croaking. Once a male frog or toad finds a mate, he climbs on her back and clings to her until she is ready to shed her eggs in the water. Then he sheds his sperm over the eggs to fertilize them. Frogs lay from 1 to 25,000 eggs at a time. Each egg has a layer of jelly. In some species the eggs (spawn) are glued together in bubbly masses. In others the eggs are laid in long strings of jelly. The spawn tends to float near the surface of the water.

The salamanders' courtship relies on smell and visual displays. In a few species of salamander the males shed their sperm into the water as frogs do. However, most male salamanders and newts produce small packets of sperm which the female picks up during courtship. The eggs are fertilized inside the female's body.

In many amphibians the eggs hatch into aquatic larvae with gills. In others, the larvae develop inside the egg until they have developed lungs. These tadpoles do not need to be in water. Sometimes, in caecilians, the young develop inside the mother's body and are born as tiny adults with lungs.

▼When the amphibian egg is released, it is surrounded by a thin layer of jelly. This swells in water, and sticks the eggs together. The jelly is slippery, and any animal wishing to eat the eggs must swallow all or none. The embryo's belly is swollen by the yolk on which it feeds.

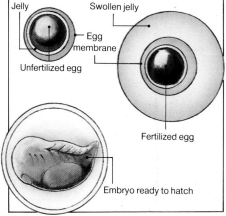

HUNTERS AND GRAZERS

Salamanders and newts feed on small invertebrates, such as insects, slugs, snails and worms. Usually they stalk their prey or lie in wait for it, then seize it in their jaws. Several salamanders can flick out their tongues to capture their prey.

Frogs and toads feed mostly on flying insects, especially gnats, mayflies, dragonflies and moths, and rely on a rapid flick of their long sticky tongue to capture food. The tongue is attached to the front of the mouth. Some species also eat large quantities of insect larvae, slugs, snails – eating the shell as well – and earthworms. The majority of adult amphibians are most active at night, when the air is moist. At night they are also less easily spotted by their enemies.

Amphibian larvae have a very wide variety of diets. Newt and salamander larvae are fierce underwater hunters, attacking smaller invertebrates. Most frog and toad tadpoles start life as vegetarians. Some filter particles of food from the water. Others scrape algae from the surfaces of underwater plants with their tiny horny teeth. As the tadpoles grow, they shed these teeth and the mouth grows wider. They gradually change to a meat diet, scavenging on dead animals or hunting smaller water animals.

HOW AMPHIBIANS BREATHE

Most adult amphibians have lungs for breathing air. They also take in oxygen through their moist skins and through the moist lining of their large mouths. Some salamanders rely entirely on this method and do not have lungs. Amphibian larvae breathe through their gills. These are fleshy feathery outgrowths with a large surface for absorbing oxygen from the water.

▲The Paradoxical frog, from Trinidad and the Amazon, gets its name because its tadpole grows up to 10in long, four times as long as the adult frog.

▼The Green salamander lives in damp crevices on rock faces. Its green coloration gives it good camouflage against a background of lichens.

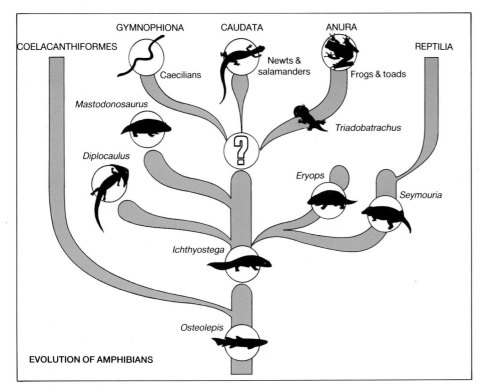

COELACANTHIFORMES

GYMNOPHIONA

Caecilians

CAUDATA

Newts &
salamanders

ANURA

Frogs & toads

REPTILIA

Mastodonosaurus

Triadobatrachus

Diplocaulus

Eryops

Seymouria

Ichthyostega

Osteolepis

EVOLUTION OF AMPHIBIANS

▲Amphibians evolved from lobe-finned fishes, relatives of the present-day coelacanth, about 370 million years ago. Modern frogs, salamanders and caecilians are different from primitive amphibians, and from each other, but the fossil record is incomplete, and we do not know exactly how they evolved.

POISONOUS PROTECTION

Amphibians have a large number of enemies. With their soft bodies they are ideal food for small mammals, birds, lizards and snakes, turtles and even larger amphibians.

The skin of most adult amphibians has poison-producing glands which make them taste bad, and may even poison a predator. Highly poisonous amphibians usually have bright warning colors so predators can learn to recognize and avoid them.

If threatened, frogs and toads may raise themselves on tiptoe and puff up their bodies so that they look much bigger than they really are. Or they may escape by diving into the water. Their bulging eyes and nostrils are situated on the top of their heads, so

they can breathe and see while the rest of the body remains hidden from view under the water.

TYPES OF AMPHIBIANS

There are three living orders and some 4,015 species of amphibians: salamanders, newts and mudpuppies (Urodela 358 species), frogs and toads (Anura 3,494 species) and caecilians (Gymnophiona 163 species).

The salamanders are the most fish-like of the amphibians. They have long flattened tails and small legs. Some species of salamander spend almost their entire lives in water. Others spend most of their adult lives on land.

Frogs and toads crawl over land in the same way as salamanders, but they can move much faster by leaping. They have long hind legs with large webbed feet, and they have no visible tails. Most adult frogs and toads spend most of the time on land.

Caecilians are strange worm-like amphibians with no legs. They live underground, and are almost blind.

ANCESTORS OF AMPHIBIANS

About 370 million years ago a group of fish, the lobe-finned fish, developed bony supports for their fins and lungs for breathing air. They were able to haul themselves out of the water on to land. Here, there were new sources of food – the insects now flourishing around the edges of the swamps. There were no large land predators to attack them, or to compete with them for food. These were the ancestors of the amphibians.

FROM WATER TO LAND

The oldest amphibian fossils are 360 million years old. Early amphibians like *Ichthyostega* show many features related to living on land instead of in water. Their skeletons had hip girdles and shoulder girdles to support the developing limbs. The skull was separated from the rest of the back by a flexible neck, allowing the head to turn when catching prey. Ribs protected the animal's soft parts as it rested on the ground. The amphibians had ears that could hear in air, eyelids to keep the eyes moist, and tongues to moisten and move food.

Some of these ancient amphibians were very large. The largest, *Mastodonosaurus*, had a skull 50in long, and was probably about 13ft long. For millions of years the amphibians ruled the world, until they were finally overcome by a newly evolved group of animals, the dinosaurs.

CAECILIANS

The loose soil on the floor of a tropical forest shifts and heaves. An animal is digging below. An earthworm emerges from the soil and starts to wriggle away. The soil still moves. Then an animal looking like a large, grayish worm breaks the surface. This is not a worm but an amphibian, a caecilian. It is pursuing the worm. It senses the worm's movements and snaps it up. Then it returns underground.

Caecilians are long-bodied, limbless amphibians with almost no tail. Most burrow in damp soil. They live in the tropics, and seem especially common in parts of Central America and West Africa, but are widespread in Asia, Africa and South America. Because caecilians are burrowers, most are very difficult to observe, and much of their life is unknown.

SKIN AND SCALES

Caecilians are very peculiar amphibians. They have no sign of limbs in their bodies. The outside of the body has rings around it, giving an earthworm-like appearance. The skin is smooth, and the outer layers are toughened with the same chemical as our fingernails are made of. The inner layer of skin has many mucus (slime) glands, and some poison glands. The poisons can hurt predators, such as snakes or birds. Unlike most amphibians, some caecilians have patches of scales on the skin, rather like those found in fish.

SOLID SKULLS

Caecilians use their heads as trowels for digging or poking in mud for food. They have very solid, bony skulls, with tough skin fitting tightly over the skull bones. They move underground by bending the body from side to side; the movement starts at the head and works backwards along the body. The curves of the body push against the soil and drive the animal forward. The rings around the body do not seem to be concerned with movement.

Caecilians eat small animals such as worms and termites. Some catch small lizards. If they can, caecilians approach their prey slowly, then grab it suddenly in their jaws. All caecilians have two rows of teeth in the upper jaw, and one or two rows in the lower. The teeth have sharp edges and are good at cutting and holding food.

▼ *Typhlonectes compressicaudata* is one of a small minority of caecilians which spend all their lives in water. Other caecilians live in water only as larvae.

CAECILIANS Order
Gymnophiona (*163 species*)

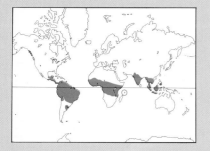

○ ◧ ☠

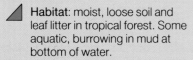

◺ **Habitat:** moist, loose soil and leaf litter in tropical forest. Some aquatic, burrowing in mud at bottom of water.

▪ **Diet:** worms, insects, other small animals.

◡ **Breeding:** some are egg-layers; others produce 7-20 live young after 9-11 month gestation. All have internal fertilization.

Size: smallest (*Idiocranium*): 3in long; longest (*Caecilia thompsoni*): 28in long. Some stout-bodied; others 100 times longer than wide.

Color: most blue-gray, some with ringing stripes, or blotched patterns.

Species mentioned in text:
Gymnophis multiplicata
Typhlonectes compressicaudata

EGGS AND BABIES

Some of the caecilians have a typical amphibian life cycle. Eggs are laid in damp places, larvae hatch and wriggle into water, then later change into adults and live the rest of their life on land. In other caecilians, larval development takes place in the egg, and a small adult hatches underground.

But in about half of the caecilians, the female produces living young. After the egg yolk is used up, the larvae remain within the mother's body feeding on "milk", secreted by glands lining the mother's oviducts. The developing babies have tiny teeth to help them feed on this milk. At birth, the babies develop adult teeth.

▲This Central American animal, *Gymnophis multiplicata*, shows the worm-like body form and covered eyes that are typical of caecilians.

▼Adult caecilians have a small tentacle on each side of the head. The tentacle is connected to the nose and is used to detect chemicals.

SALAMANDERS

It is a dark, rainy evening. From beneath a mossy log a tiny salamander emerges. Tonight the salamander is unlucky. It is seized by a small snake. But the salamander's skin produces so much sticky slime that the snake lets go.

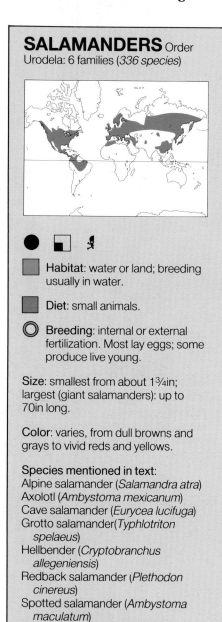

SALAMANDERS Order
Urodela: 6 families (*336 species*)

● ◼ ☠

◼ Habitat: water or land; breeding usually in water.

◼ Diet: small animals.

○ Breeding: internal or external fertilization. Most lay eggs; some produce live young.

Size: smallest from about 1¾in; largest (giant salamanders): up to 70in long.

Color: varies, from dull browns and grays to vivid reds and yellows.

Species mentioned in text:
Alpine salamander (*Salamandra atra*)
Axolotl (*Ambystoma mexicanum*)
Cave salamander (*Eurycea lucifuga*)
Grotto salamander(*Typhlotriton spelaeus*)
Hellbender (*Cryptobranchus allegeniensis*)
Redback salamander (*Plethodon cinereus*)
Spotted salamander (*Ambystoma maculatum*)
Texas blind salamander (*Typhlomolge rathbuni*)
Two-lined salamander (*Eurycea bislineata*).

Salamanders, newts, and their relatives make up the amphibian order Urodela. They have long bodies, long tails, and two pairs of legs of roughly similar size. Most are found in temperate climates in North America, Europe and Asia, but some live in the tropics of Central and South America.

There are nine different families of the Urodela. Six are dealt with here. Later pages in this book deal with Congo eels and sirens (see pages 18-19) and mudpuppies (see pages 20-21). A few species of salamander are commonly given the name "newt;" these are described on pages 16-17.

WATERY HOMES

Salamanders live in a wide variety of habitats. Some species live entirely on land, some live entirely in water, while others divide their time between land and water. The skin of a salamander allows water to pass through quite easily. Because of this, even the land types need to live in damp places. If they are exposed to hot dry conditions, they soon lose water and die. Land-living species

▲The axolotl usually spends all its life in water, and keeps larval features such as the feathery gills. Some forms are albino.

commonly live under rocks and logs or burrow in damp earth. In very hot weather, salamanders retreat into damp refuges, emerging only during the cool of the night. But, like other amphibians, they are a similar temperature to their surroundings. If temperatures are too low, they hide away and become inactive.

BREATHING SKINS

Many salamanders breathe air using lungs. A salamander may also use the damp inner surface of its mouth to get oxygen. Often the soft skin under the salamander's throat can be seen pumping rapidly, helping to change the air in the mouth.

Even when these two methods are used, quite a large part of a salamander's oxygen is obtained through the damp skin. The largest family of salamanders, with over 200 species, do not have lungs at all. They breathe just through the mouth and skin.

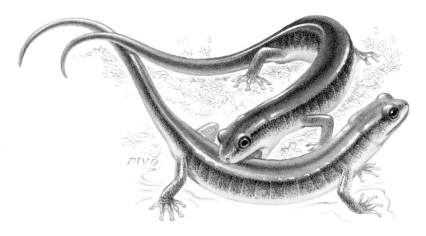

▼The Cave salamander spends all its life on land. It lives in the twilight zone near cave entrances.

▲Many male salamanders bite or grasp the female during courtship, as do Two-lined salamanders.

REPULSIVE SKINS

In a salamander's skin there are many glands. Some of these help to keep it moist and slimy. But some species have other glands that secrete substances which are poisonous or taste nasty. These can deter enemy attacks.

Poisonous salamanders are often very brightly colored to warn predators to leave them alone. Several species, such as the Spotted salamander, have glands on the back of the neck. When attacked, they crouch to present their bad-tasting neck to the enemy. Others with glands on the neck actually butt an enemy with their heads. Some of the American mole

salamanders do this. It seems effective against small predators such as shrews. Some lungless salamanders have many glands on the tail. When attacked, they wave the tail at an enemy. They may be able to shed their tails, leaving behind a distasteful morsel which thrashes wildly and distracts the predator. The salamanders can then escape and grow a new tail.

SMALL APPETITES

All salamanders are carnivores. They feed on small living animals such as insects, slugs, snails and worms. Some kinds can flick out the tongue to catch prey. Salamanders can be quite ferocious for their size, but because of their slow pace of life and periods of inactivity they do not consume huge amounts of food. The slow pace of their lives may also help them become long-lived. Quite small species may live 25 years, and some individuals are known to have lived 50 years.

HIDDEN MILLIONS

Salamanders are secretive. Most are small (few are more than 6in long), live in cool shady places, and become active at night, so they usually escape human attention. But in some places they can be very abundant. In the forests of eastern USA, it has been calculated that there is probably a greater weight of salamanders than all the birds and mammals put together.

BIGGEST AMPHIBIANS

Some salamanders are the biggest of all living amphibians. These are the giant salamanders of eastern Asia. As much as 5¼ft in length, they never leave the water, which supports their weight. They breathe with lungs and through the skin.

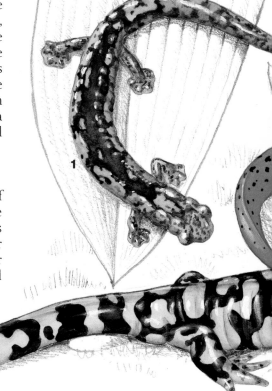

▲Species of salamander *Bolitoglossa schizodactyla* (**1**) is a lungless species with webbed feet. The Red salamander (*Pseudotriton ruber*) (**2**) burrows into mud near streams. The Tiger salamander (*Ambystoma tigrinum*) (**3**) is a close relative of the axolotl. *Batrachuperus pinchonii* (**4**) and *Onychodactylus japonicus* (**5**) live in Asia. *Tylototriton taliangensis* (**6**) has a warty skin.

◄The Spotted salamander of North America lives on land as an adult, but returns to water to lay its eggs.

EGGS AND NESTS

Salamanders have three main types of life cycle. Some breed entirely on land. Some have a "typical" amphibian life cycle, with eggs and larvae in the water and adults on land. (Newts are a good example of this.) Then there are species that spend all the stages of their life cycle in water.

The Redback salamander, found in woodland areas of eastern North America, is a wholly land-living species. After mating, the female lays 20-30

eggs in a rotten log. The eggs are large, and the embryos inside them develop fast. The whole larval development is passed within the egg so the hatching salamander is just a tiny version of the adult. In some salamanders, such as the Alpine salamander of Europe, the egg develops inside the mother, who gives birth to live young.

In salamanders that live entirely in water, the number of eggs laid is often high. The hellbender of America lays up to 450 eggs. The male hellbender digs out a nest and guards it. He allows females to lay their eggs in the nest, then he fertilizes them, and guards them for the 10-12 weeks they take to develop into larvae. The larvae leave the nest and fend for themselves.

STAYING YOUNG

In various species of some families, such as the mole salamanders, gills and other larval features can be kept throughout life. Sometimes populations of the same species develop

differently in different environments. One population may progress to the adult in the normal way. Another population may keep large, frilly gills and a flattened tail. It seems to depend on the living conditions. But these "larval" forms may be able to reproduce. The most famous example is the axolotl of Mexico, which is typically larval looking, but can change to an "adult" if given the chemical iodine. Other species will change into adults if the water they are living in dries up.

▲ The hellbender is the largest of the North American salamanders, reaching 28in from snout to tail.

BLIND CAVE-DWELLERS

Some of the lungless salamanders live in underground water in caves. The Texas blind salamander is white, with tiny eyes. The Grotto salamander, of the Ozarks in the USA, has a gray or brown larva which lives in streams, but the adult retreats into caves and loses its color and the use of its eyes.

NEWTS

It is breeding time in spring. A male newt swims in front of the smaller female and blocks her way. He lashes his tail towards her, hitting her with a stream of water. He keeps up this courtship "dance" for some while. Then he deposits a packet of sperm on the pond bottom. It is picked up by the female and mating is complete.

▼**Newt courtship** The eft or young (1) of the Red-spotted newt is red all over. The adults (2) are duller, with characteristic red spots. The male rubs a cheek gland on the female as he courts her. A breeding male Smooth newt (3) has dark spots, stripes on the head, a crest on the tail and body, and fringed hind toes.

NEWTS Salamandridae
(*53 species*)

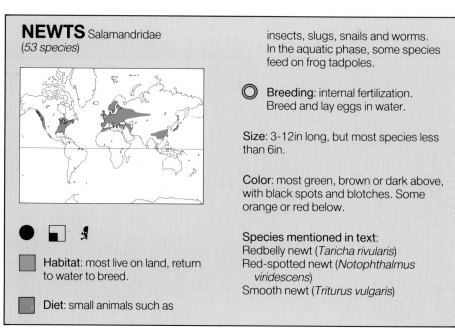

● ◨ 🗡

◻ **Habitat:** most live on land, return to water to breed.

◻ **Diet:** small animals such as insects, slugs, snails and worms. In the aquatic phase, some species feed on frog tadpoles.

◎ **Breeding:** internal fertilization. Breed and lay eggs in water.

Size: 3-12in long, but most species less than 6in.

Color: most green, brown or dark above, with black spots and blotches. Some orange or red below.

Species mentioned in text:
Redbelly newt (*Taricha rivularis*)
Red-spotted newt (*Notophthalmus viridescens*)
Smooth newt (*Triturus vulgaris*)

Newts all belong to the salamander family Salamandridae. There is no special scientific distinction between newts and salamanders, but "newt" is a common name given to several members of this family which live on land and return to the water for a few weeks in spring to breed.

HOMING CLUES
During their land-living stage, newts may be found several miles from a pond suitable for breeding. They can find their way back to their "home" waters, often the ones in which they

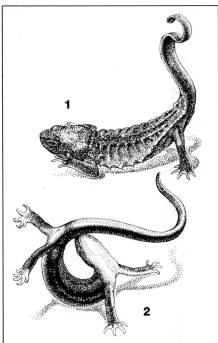

grew up, using clues of various kinds. They all use their senses of smell and sight for direction-finding, but some newts have unusual senses. A number of species navigate by the Sun; others, such as the American Red-spotted newt, can use the Earth's magnetism to check their direction.

WATERY CHANGES
In their land-living phase, newts are generally inconspicuous, and spend much of their time in hiding places. They are often easier to find in water during the breeding season. They may undergo quite a change in appearance between the seasons. On land, the long body and tail are rounded. In the water, the skin becomes thinner and easier to breathe through. The tail becomes deep and flattened to help with swimming. Colors, especially of males, may become more vivid. Males of some species also develop a large body crest. Apart from showing its

◀ **Defensive postures** The Spiny newt (*Echinotriton andersoni*) **(1)** in defensive posture. It has long spiny ribs. If grasped by a predator, these push out through poison glands in the skin. A Redbelly newt **(2)** holds tail and chin high to show the warning color below.

▼ **Other courtship behavior** The male Redbelly **(1)** clasps the female and rubs a gland under his chin on her nostrils. The male Smooth newt **(2)** fans his tail to send odors to the female.

owner is male, this crest may help to increase the surface area which can absorb oxygen during the active courtship. In the skin, lateral line organs like those of fish develop. These are able to detect movements of prey in the water. Even the eyes change slightly to focus underwater.

COURTSHIP DANCES
In newts, fertilization is internal, but the male has no penis to insert in the female during mating. Instead he produces a little packet of sperm sitting on a base, like a golf ball on a tee. He has to persuade the female to walk over this and take the packet from the "tee" into her cloaca. An elaborate courtship dance may be used to maneuver her into the right position. Sometimes the male may grab the female, as in the Redbelly newt. Secretions from scent glands are important parts of the ritual.

EGGS AND YOUNG
The females of all European species usually lay their eggs singly on water plants. The eggs hatch into larvae, which have feathery gills. Legs form later. Further on in summer, the gills disappear and the tiny newts (efts) emerge on to land. In some species, they may spend several years on land before returning to water to breed.

CONGO EELS AND SIRENS

The mud at the bottom of a ditch stirs. A head appears, fringed with frilly gills, followed by a long, dark body. The siren wriggles lazily across the mud, with no apparent aim. But it is approaching a crayfish from behind, and before this animal can escape, the siren's jaws snap shut to capture it.

There are three species of Congo eel, or amphiuma, and three species of siren. All are long-bodied and completely aquatic. They live in North America. Congo eels have lungs, and four legs, although the legs are too tiny to be of any use in the adults. The sirens have gills on the outside of the body, and no back legs. The weak front legs are just behind the head.

MUDDY HOMES
Congo eels are swamp-dwellers. After rain, they may sometimes wriggle out at the water's edge. Usually, though, they are out of sight, living in a burrow from which they emerge at night to feed on frogs, snails and fish. Sirens live in ditches, shallow streams and lakes, but they too spend much of their time buried in the sand or mud at the bottom of the water.

SURVIVING DROUGHT
Many of the ponds and ditches where sirens live dry up in the summer. As the sand or mud dries out, the slime coat on the siren's skin hardens to form a stiff cocoon, which covers its whole body except the mouth. It can survive like this for many weeks until the water returns.

GUARDING THE EGGS
Congo eels lay a long string of eggs. The mother coils round them and guards them until they hatch, which can be 20 weeks or more. Egg-laying often happens when water levels are high. As it falls, the female and her eggs may be left in a damp hollow beneath a log. When they hatch, the young find their way back to water.

BIG AND SMALL
The Three-toed amphiuma, and the Greater siren, can reach lengths of up to 36in, making them some of the largest amphibians. Big Congo eels can give a painful bite. At the other extreme is the Dwarf siren, only about 4in long, which thrives among water hyacinths.

CONGO EELS AND SIRENS Amphiumidae and Sirenidae (*6 species*)

● ▣

≋ Habitat: live entirely in water.

▥ Diet: frogs, fish, worms, snails.

◎ Breeding: internal fertilization in Congo eels, which lay up to 200 eggs. Siren breeding little known; eggs laid singly.

Size: 4-43in long.

Color: dull colors, browns, blacks, grays and greens.

Species mentioned in text:
Dwarf siren (*Pseudobranchus striatus*)
Greater siren (*Siren lacertina*)
Three-toed amphiuma or Congo eel
(*Amphiuma tridactylum*)

▶A Congo eel in its watery home. These animals have long thin bodies, but are amphibians, not fish. All live in southeastern USA, not in Africa.

MUDPUPPIES

Deep in an underground cavern, a cold stream runs beneath the earth. It is totally dark. But the water is not empty of life. In a backwater floats a salamander as long as a man's hand. It is too dark to see, but this animal feels its way through the water and detects its prey without using eyes. But it feels no movement of other animals now. It sinks to the bottom and rests on the cavern floor. Much of its time is spent resting.

The animals in the mudpuppy family live their lives completely in water. Even as breeding adults they keep the feathery gills of larvae, and have small, weak legs. In eastern North America live the mudpuppy and the water-dogs. These names were given in the false belief that these animals bark. In Europe, in Yugoslavia and one small area of Italy, lives the olm.

POT-HOLING SALAMANDER

Olms live entirely in caves, often far underground. Up to 12in long, including tail, they live in pitch darkness in caves with temperatures between 41 and 50°F. Occasionally, when there are floods, olms may be swept from their caves into open waters. Otherwise they are rarely seen by people. Olms seem to be becoming rarer, perhaps because of pollution.

A DARK WORLD

Skin color is of no importance in the darkness. The olm has no pigment, so looks a pasty white, except for the gills, which are bright red where the blood shows through. Eyes are also of little use in the darkness, and those of the olm are very tiny.

BREEDING MYSTERY

Olms, as studied in aquaria, seem to have two ways of producing young. Whether both are used in the wild, or whether one is the normal method, is not really known. Sometimes the female lays eggs, in a clutch of up to 70, beneath a stone. Both male and female seem to guard them as they develop.

Alternatively, the female may keep her eggs inside her body. Most eggs break down, providing nourishment for just two, which develop into large larvae and are born alive. Young olms may show some signs of coloring, but this usually disappears before they are adult. If exposed to light, they may become colored. The olm is quite variable both in size and shape. This is

MUDPUPPIES Proteidae
(6 species)

● ◰ ☠

⌇ Habitat: live entirely in water.

▮ Diet: frogs, fish, worms, snails.

◎ Breeding: internal fertilization. Up to 190 eggs laid. Olm may produce live young.

Size: 4½-13in long.

Color: dull colors, gray or brown. Olm white.

Species mentioned in text:
Mudpuppy (Necturus maculosus)
Olm (Proteus anguinus)
Waterdog (Necturus lewisi)

▲The olm (1) lives in underground streams and lakes in caves in Yugoslavia. It is usually white, but young ones may show some color. The mudpuppy (2) lives in North America in ponds, lakes and streams.

▶A mudpuppy shows its blood-filled external gills. The gills vary in size depending on the oxygen content of the water. In stagnant water they are large, but in running water, where there is much oxygen, they may be quite small.

▼A waterdog scrambles over a dead log. Although they breathe mainly by gills, these animals sometimes come to the surface for air, or even emerge briefly on land if the soil is damp.

perhaps not surprising, as the populations in different caves and regions are unable to mix, and are likely to pass on their own peculiarities to their offspring.

DOGGED DEVOTION

In the mudpuppies and waterdogs, mating takes place in the fall. The eggs are fertilized internally, but remain inside the mother until the next spring. The female lays up to 190 eggs, sticking each to a rock or a log. The eggs are guarded for between 5 and 9 weeks. The male performs this task, which makes a long devotion to duty for an animal that mated months before. Mudpuppies take several years to reach maturity. They feed on fish, insects and crayfish.

FROGS AND TOADS

It is a rainy night in early spring. From a pond comes a sound like small motor-bike engines – male frogs calling to advertise their presence. Other frogs hop to the pond from all directions. The large females, full of eggs, are seized by males as they enter the water. Next morning, the pond is full of round masses of frogspawn.

Frogs and toads are the most numerous amphibians. They are found on most islands and on all continents except Antarctica. The great majority occur in warm areas of the world, but many are found in cool climates. Two species, the European common frog and the Wood frog of North America, can even live within the Arctic Circle. Most frogs and toads live both in water and on land, at least for part

FROGS AND TOADS
Order Anura: 17 families
(*2,609 species*)

● ◨ ⚏

◤ **Habitat:** adults live mostly on land. Some burrow or climb. Some live entirely in water.

▢ **Diet:** insects, worms, snails, some small vertebrates.

◎ **Breeding:** typically external

fertilization, laying eggs in water where tadpoles develop. Many variations and exceptions.

Size: smallest (*Sminthillus limbatus*): ½in snout to vent; largest (Goliath frog): 10in.

Color: from dull browns and greens to vivid reds, yellows, blues.

Species mentioned in text:
Darwin's frog (*Rhinoderma darwinii*)
European common frog (*Rana temporaria*)
Golden toad (*Bufo periglenes*)
Goliath frog (*Rana goliath*)
Malaysian horned toad (*Ceratophrys dorsata*)
Midwife toad (*Alytes obstetricans*)
Red-and-blue dart-poison frog (*Dendrobates pumilio*)
Surinam toad (*Pipa pipa*)
Western spadefoot toad (*Scaphiopus hammondii*)
Wood frog (*Rana sylvatica*)

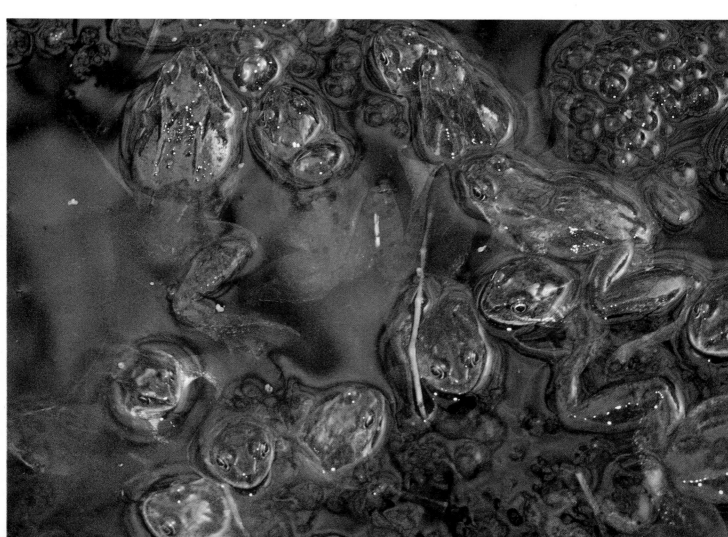

of their lives, but some live entirely in water and others entirely on land. Some succeed in living in places that seem at first sight unsuitable, such as savannahs and deserts.

FROG OR TOAD?

How can frogs be told from toads? "Frogs" are smooth-skinned, long-limbed and live in or close to water. "Toads" are stout-bodied with short limbs, and have warty skins. They live in damp places away from water. The word frog or toad really describes the look of the creature. There is no special scientific difference. Some scientific families contain both "frogs" and "toads." In this book the tree frogs are dealt with on pages 28 to 31. All other frogs and toads are dealt with in this section. Unless a particular type is specified, the term "frog" includes toads as well.

LONG JUMP EXPERTS

Frogs have a much shorter body than other amphibians. They have nine bones or less in the backbone, which makes it short and rigid. Frogs do not have a narrow neck so the head joins straight on to the body. They do not have a tail either.

These adaptations are connected with the way frogs jump. The long back legs fold into three sections, thigh, shin and foot, of almost equal length. When the leg is suddenly straightened, the frog shoots forward. The short front limbs cushion the landing. The direction of jump is not always very well controlled, but it makes an effective means of escaping an enemy. The record for a single leap by a large frog is 16½ft; most jumps are much shorter. The long back limbs are also good for swimming. They are pushed backwards in an action similar to the human breaststroke, and the webbed feet push on the water.

Some species of frog are good burrowers. They dig themselves down backwards using a sideways shuffle of the hind feet. The heel in these species has a special hard projection that acts as a scraper and shovel.

BIG EYES AND EARS

A frog's eyes are usually large. They are at the side of the head, so the frog can watch all round for danger. Some kinds of frog have eyes that are specially adapted to detect small moving objects which might be prey. The eyes have lids to protect them, and

▼ Many species of frog gather in large numbers at spawning sites. These are spawning European common frogs.

▼ Mating Golden toads. During mating, the male clasps the female and fertilizes the eggs as she lays them.

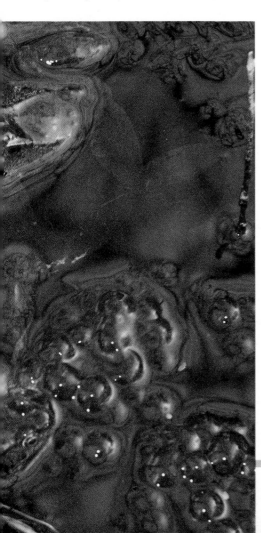

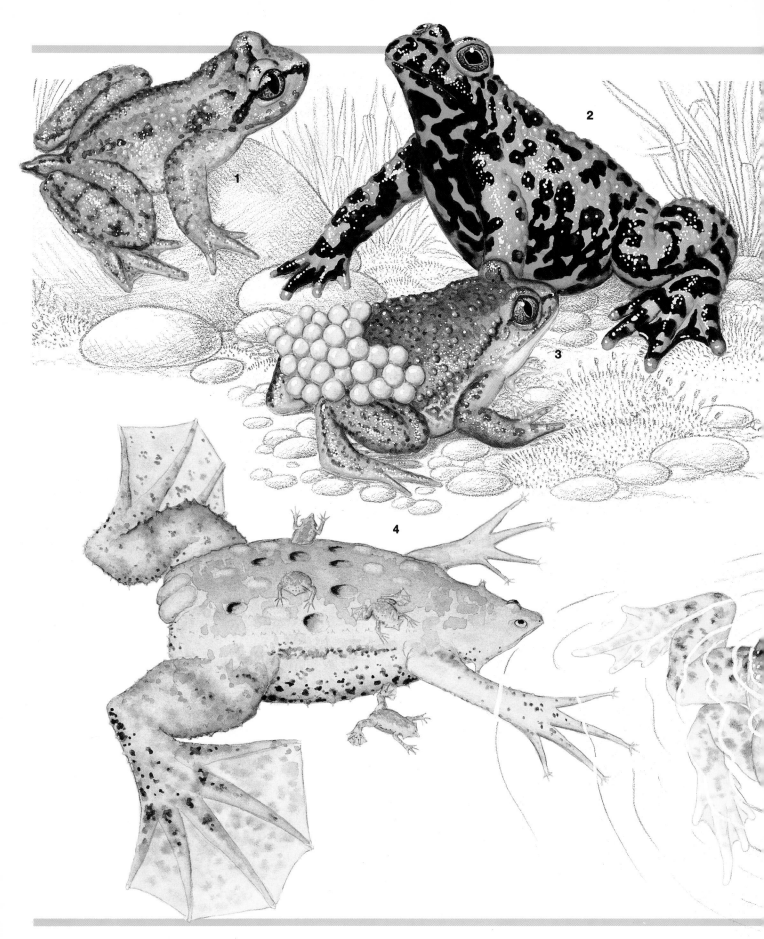

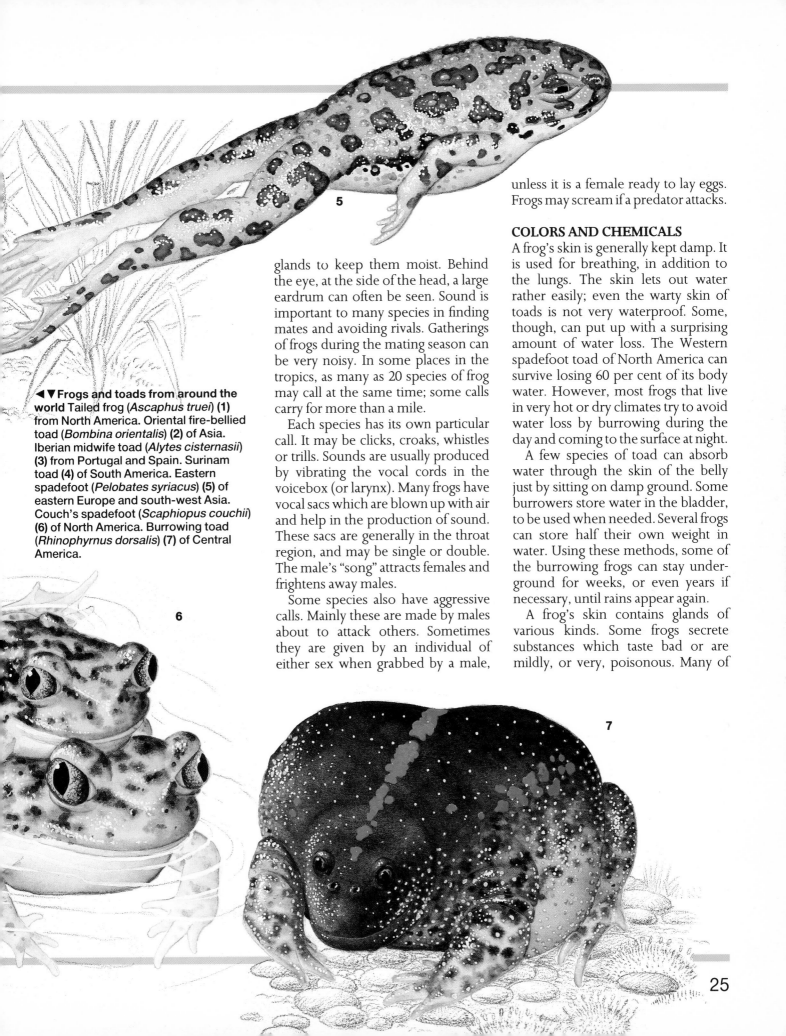

◄▼**Frogs and toads from around the world** Tailed frog (*Ascaphus truei*) **(1)** from North America. Oriental fire-bellied toad (*Bombina orientalis*) **(2)** of Asia. Iberian midwife toad (*Alytes cisternasii*) **(3)** from Portugal and Spain. Surinam toad **(4)** of South America. Eastern spadefoot (*Pelobates syriacus*) **(5)** of eastern Europe and south-west Asia. Couch's spadefoot (*Scaphiopus couchii*) **(6)** of North America. Burrowing toad (*Rhinophyrnus dorsalis*) **(7)** of Central America.

glands to keep them moist. Behind the eye, at the side of the head, a large eardrum can often be seen. Sound is important to many species in finding mates and avoiding rivals. Gatherings of frogs during the mating season can be very noisy. In some places in the tropics, as many as 20 species of frog may call at the same time; some calls carry for more than a mile.

Each species has its own particular call. It may be clicks, croaks, whistles or trills. Sounds are usually produced by vibrating the vocal cords in the voicebox (or larynx). Many frogs have vocal sacs which are blown up with air and help in the production of sound. These sacs are generally in the throat region, and may be single or double. The male's "song" attracts females and frightens away males.

Some species also have aggressive calls. Mainly these are made by males about to attack others. Sometimes they are given by an individual of either sex when grabbed by a male, unless it is a female ready to lay eggs. Frogs may scream if a predator attacks.

COLORS AND CHEMICALS

A frog's skin is generally kept damp. It is used for breathing, in addition to the lungs. The skin lets out water rather easily; even the warty skin of toads is not very waterproof. Some, though, can put up with a surprising amount of water loss. The Western spadefoot toad of North America can survive losing 60 per cent of its body water. However, most frogs that live in very hot or dry climates try to avoid water loss by burrowing during the day and coming to the surface at night.

A few species of toad can absorb water through the skin of the belly just by sitting on damp ground. Some burrowers store water in the bladder, to be used when needed. Several frogs can store half their own weight in water. Using these methods, some of the burrowing frogs can stay underground for weeks, or even years if necessary, until rains appear again.

A frog's skin contains glands of various kinds. Some frogs secrete substances which taste bad or are mildly, or very, poisonous. Many of the most poisonous frogs, such as the dart-poison frogs of Central and South America, are decked out in brilliant colors that may serve to warn off enemies. Other frogs may have "flash" colors that suddenly show when they jump, and may confuse a predator. Most frogs, though, have subdued colors which work well to camouflage them. Some, such as the Malaysian horned toad, go one stage better by having bodies which imitate the shape and color of dead leaves on the forest floor where they live.

MASS BREEDING

Most frogs are scattered over a wide area for much of the year, and must migrate to a suitable breeding site when conditions are right. Hundreds, or even thousands of individuals, may congregate in one spot. Frogs will often return to the same pond or lake again and again, often the one in which they grew up. They may even pass other apparently suitable water on the way there.

Many kinds of clues and landmarks seem to be involved in this navigation. Unfortunately, frogs may continue to return to places ruined as breeding sites by man. They may also cross roads and railways and be killed in large numbers. In some places in Britain "toad tunnels" have been built under roads so they can cross the road in safety.

FROM EGG TO FROG

The typical frog lays large numbers of eggs coated with jelly in the water. The tadpoles that hatch from the eggs have a rounded body containing feeding organs, with a long, coiled gut for digesting plant food. They have gills to breathe, and a long tail which they wriggle to help them swim. After some weeks growing, they "metamorphose." Legs grow. The tail is lost. Gills disappear. Lungs form. The long gut becomes much shorter, and now copes with a diet of insects and other small animals. They are now frogs, and live mainly on land. This is the typical frog life cycle.

Many species of frog have more unusual ways of growing up. Some frogs lay their eggs on vegetation in a nest of frothy foam that hardens like meringue. At hatching time, the foam softens, and the tadpoles drop into the water below.

Some species produce fewer eggs, but look after them so that they stand a better chance of survival. In the Midwife toad, the male winds the string of eggs round his hind legs and carries them about. He takes the eggs to water for hatching. Some species of dart-poison frog put a single tadpole into a tiny pond formed at the leaf base of a plant. The mother lays a clutch of unfertilized eggs to act as food for the tadpole.

The female Surinam toad keeps the eggs embedded in the skin of the back until they develop into tiny toads. Perhaps the oddest of all is Darwin's frog, in which the male swallows hatching tadpoles into his large vocal sac. When they have completed their development there, he spits them out as froglets.

◄Oriental fire-bellied toads are camouflaged above, but display the bright belly colors when attacked.

►Warning colors are found in many frogs, such as these Red-and-blue dart-poison frogs.

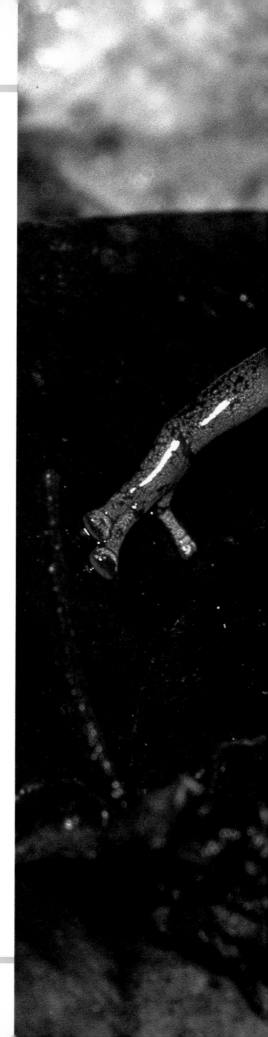

TREE FROGS

The reeds at the edge of the pond seem empty. But as a swarm of gnats dances over the water, the reeds erupt in movement. Little green shapes launch themselves into the air after the flying meals. The pond edge is full of hungry young tree frogs, clambering on the plants and watching for easy prey.

There are tree frogs living over most of the warmer parts of the world. The true tree frogs are a large family with over 600 species. They are widespread in many countries with a warm climate but absent from most of Africa and southern Asia. There they are replaced by the Old World tree frogs, which include the "flying" frogs. A third small family of tree frogs lives in tropical America. These are the glass frogs, generally bright green, but with such a transparent skin that many of their bones and organs can be seen from outside.

TACKY TOES

Tree frogs often have rather flattened bodies. This helps them keep balance and they can press close to leaves or tree trunks when they are resting. The flat skin of the belly is loose and can be pressed tightly against a surface to help them stick. Many tree frogs have large areas of sticky webbing between their fingers and toes which also help them hold on. The toes end in round discs which act as suckers, allowing

the frog to climb up smooth leaves. Many tree frogs also have extra bones in their toes which help them to curl the toes round very thin twigs to get a grip. All this, together with their small size and lightness, makes them very agile climbers.

The eyes of many tree frogs are very large. They often face forward more than the eyes of other frogs. Both these features help them to judge distances as they jump and climb, and

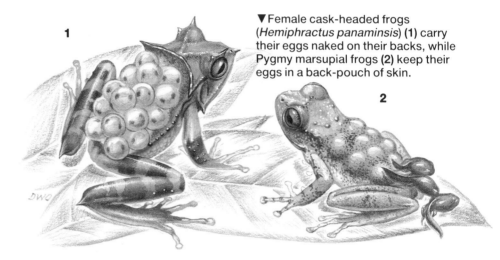

▼Female cask-headed frogs (*Hemiphractus panaminsis*) **(1)** carry their eggs naked on their backs, while Pygmy marsupial frogs **(2)** keep their eggs in a back-pouch of skin.

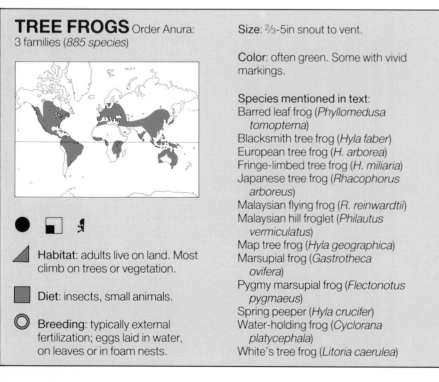

TREE FROGS Order Anura:
3 families (*885 species*)

Size: ⅔-5in snout to vent.

Color: often green. Some with vivid markings.

Species mentioned in text:
Barred leaf frog (*Phyllomedusa tomopterna*)
Blacksmith tree frog (*Hyla faber*)
European tree frog (*H. arborea*)
Fringe-limbed tree frog (*H. miliaria*)
Japanese tree frog (*Rhacophorus arboreus*)
Malaysian flying frog (*R. reinwardtii*)
Malaysian hill froglet (*Philautus vermiculatus*)
Map tree frog (*Hyla geographica*)
Marsupial frog (*Gastrotheca ovifera*)
Pygmy marsupial frog (*Flectonotus pygmaeus*)
Spring peeper (*Hyla crucifer*)
Water-holding frog (*Cyclorana platycephala*)
White's tree frog (*Litoria caerulea*)

● ◼ ⍦

◣ **Habitat:** adults live on land. Most climb on trees or vegetation.

◼ **Diet:** insects, small animals.

◯ **Breeding:** typically external fertilization; eggs laid in water, on leaves or in foam nests.

▲ Tropical leaf frogs, for example *Phyllomedusa bicolor*, lay their eggs wrapped in leaves overhanging water.

► A shoal of tadpoles of the Map tree frog in Trinidad may gain safety from predators by clumping.

also when attacking prey. Most are active at night, and large eyes may operate well at low light levels. Many insects are active at night, giving the frogs their main food supply.

FLYING FROGS

In the jungles of South-east Asia live several species of "flying" frogs. Flying frogs have even bigger feet than most tree frogs, and long toes with well-developed webs between the toes. They can jump from a tree, spread the webbing, and parachute safely to a lower level. A Malaysian flying frog may travel 50ft or so in a single glide from one tree to another. The Fringe-limbed tree frog of Central America has similar habits.

Some species have the ability to change color greatly. The Malaysian flying frog may change color through the day from blue to green to black.

▼ A European tree frog springs from its perch. They sometimes leap to catch food, but the usual reason is to escape from their enemies.

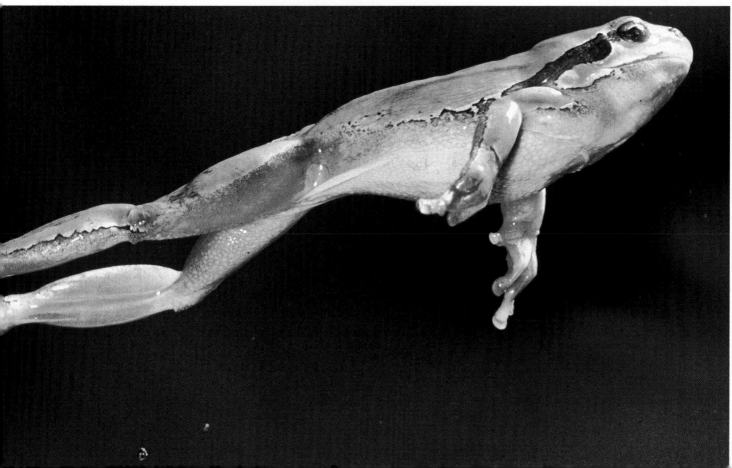

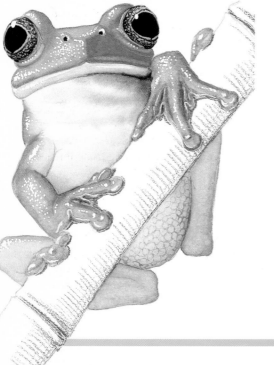

▲ The Barred leaf frog lives in the Amazon rain forest. The huge eyes are a major sense, especially for hunting.

◄ The green coloring of the Japanese tree frog is good camouflage when the animal is among leaves.

UNDERGROUND TREE FROGS

Not all of the tree frog family spend their time climbing. Some of the group have become ground-living, including the cricket frogs of North America, in which the toe discs are quite small. A few even go underground. The Water-holding frog of Australia is one. It lives in very dry regions. When it can get water it drinks until it is bloated. It secretes a special outer skin layer, which helps prevent water loss. This allows it to survive the lengthy dry periods by burrowing into the soil with its own water store. When rains come, these frogs may emerge in their thousands to breed. Trains on the Australian transcontinental railway have on occasions had to stop because so many frogs were squashed on the lines, the wheels could not get a grip.

Australia has a variety of tree frogs, some beautifully colored. They can be pink, blue, violet, yellow or even shiny. Probably the best known is White's tree frog, which often finds its way into houses, water tanks and drainpipes. Like many tree frogs, this species is green, although its scientific name means sky-blue. It was named from a pickled specimen which had lost the yellow color from its skin.

NOISY SINGERS

Several species of tree frog are noisy breeders, producing loud calls to attract mates to the breeding pond. American species such as the Spring peeper are very well known for their choruses. The Spring peeper blows the floor of its mouth out as a huge resonating chamber. Calling males of the European tree frog are sometimes mistaken for quacking ducks.

Many tree frogs lay clumps of spawn in the water and tadpoles develop into adults in typical frog fashion. In some kinds, such as the European tree frog, the tadpoles are rather solitary. In others, large numbers of tadpoles may clump together. Sometimes these shoals swim in a spiral. The action may stir up food from the bottom of the pond.

PRIVATE POND

The Blacksmith tree frog of South America comes to the ground in the breeding season. The male finds shallow water and makes a nest of mud. This is shaped like a crater, with walls about 4in high, and collects its own little pool of water. The male sits there until he has attracted a female to lay her eggs. The tadpoles are thus provided with their own private pond, giving them a safer start to life.

LEAF NESTS

The leaf frogs are mostly large and brightly colored. They live in wet forest in Central and South America. During mating, they hold leaves together, and lay their eggs between the leaves. The sticky, stiff jelly around the eggs keeps the leaves together until the first tadpoles hatch, when the jelly softens and the tadpoles drop in the water. The female may keep the developing eggs moist by repeatedly emptying her bladder over them.

Many of the Old World tree frogs are foam nesters. Several males may compete to fertilize the eggs as the female lays them, and the males'

▲ *Hyla leucophyllata* of South America shows the toe pads which tree frogs use to cling to leaves and vertical surfaces.

▼ Tiny froglets of the Marsupial frog emerge from their mother's pouch, their development completed without water.

thrashing legs beat the foam into a nest. Such a nest may contain up to as many as 150 eggs.

Glass frogs usually lay their eggs on leaves above water. In some species they are known to be guarded by the male. The Malaysian hill froglet lives high in the cloud forests where there are few pools of water. It lays its eggs in huge sheets of damp moss hanging from trees. The eggs develop directly into miniature froglets.

TADPOLE BACKPACKS

In about 60 species of tropical tree frogs, the female lays a fairly small number of eggs which she then carries on her back. They may just be stuck to the skin. In others there is an open pouch in the skin to carry the eggs.

The female Pygmy marsupial frog of South America has an open pouch on her back in which the eggs develop. She releases the tadpoles into little pools formed at the base of the leaves of some plants.

The female Marsupial frog has a pouch on her back which can be closed. She lays eggs with her back up and head downwards. The male fertilizes the eggs and they slip down a groove into the pouch. The tadpoles continue their development riding in the pouch. Their movements can be seen as they wriggle about. The tadpoles emerge as froglets, having been protected for the most vulnerable part of their life. When it is time for them to emerge, the mother opens the pouch entrance with her longest toe.

WHAT IS A REPTILE?

Snakes, crocodiles, lizards, tortoises and turtles are all reptiles. Their skin is covered in horny scales, and they are vertebrates: they have an internal bony skeleton with a central backbone. Most species spend all their lives on land. Reptiles are ectothermic (cold-blooded); their body temperature depends on the temperature of their immediate surroundings.

Reptiles are better adapted to life on land than amphibians. Their scaly skin prevents their bodies from drying out. Even more important, they reproduce by laying eggs protected by shells, or by giving birth to live young. There is no free-living larva stage. Reptiles excrete uric acid – a solid waste that does not require water in order to be eliminated from the body.

TYPES OF REPTILES

There are four main categories, or orders, of reptiles:

Turtles are covered in a heavy shell. They have a horny beak instead of teeth, and there are no openings in the back of the skull (244 species).

Lizards, snakes and worm-lizards all evolved from ancestors that had two pairs of legs, and some still have pelvic girdles in their skeletons. They all have a movable bone linking the lower jaw to the skull, which allows for relatively free movement of the jaw. Snakes have very long backbones, and can unhinge their jaws to swallow large prey. Worm-lizards live underground, and have no legs. They have heavy skulls for burrowing, and are almost blind (lizards, 3,751 species; snakes, 2,389 species; worm-lizards, 140 species).

Crocodiles and alligators spend much of their lives in water, where they use their powerful flattened tails for swimming. They are covered in horny plates strengthened with bone,

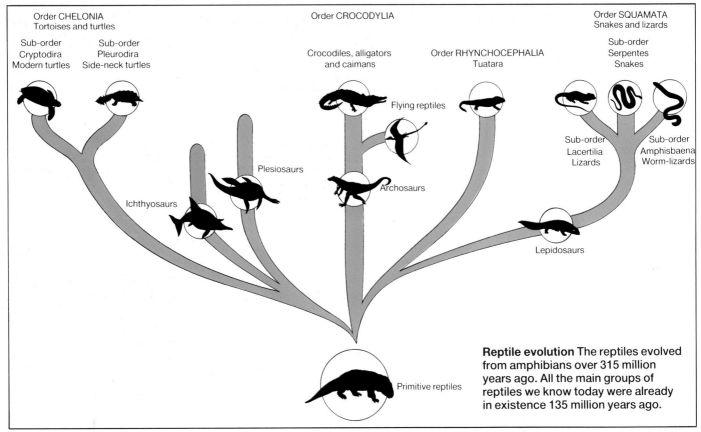

Order CHELONIA
Tortoises and turtles

Sub-order
Cryptodira
Modern turtles

Sub-order
Pleurodira
Side-neck turtles

Order CROCODYLIA

Crocodiles, alligators
and caimans

Order RHYNCHOCEPHALIA
Tuatara

Flying reptiles

Order SQUAMATA
Snakes and lizards

Sub-order
Serpentes
Snakes

Sub-order
Lacertilia
Lizards

Sub-order
Amphisbaena
Worm-lizards

Plesiosaurs

Archosaurs

Ichthyosaurs

Lepidosaurs

Primitive reptiles

Reptile evolution The reptiles evolved from amphibians over 315 million years ago. All the main groups of reptiles we know today were already in existence 135 million years ago.

which extend all around their bodies, and a crest of horny plates on their tails. Their eyes and nostrils are raised so that they can protrude above the water while the rest of the animal is submerged (22 species).

The tuatara is the only living member of an ancient order of reptiles. It has a third "eye" on the top of the head, which is sensitive to light. It has two upper rows of teeth, one row on the upper jaw and one row on the palate. The lower teeth fit between these two rows. A crest of horny plates runs along its back (1 species).

AGE OF REPTILES
Reptiles evolved from amphibians millions of years ago, by slowly developing eggs with shells and a waterproof covering of scales. The earliest fossil reptiles have been found in rocks of the Carboniferous period, about 315 million years old. By this time many different types of reptiles had evolved, including the dinosaurs, so they probably arose even earlier.

Their shelled eggs allowed them to live far away from water, and by the Permian period, 280 million years ago, they were found in large numbers almost all over the Earth.

In this Age of Reptiles, these animals were the dominant creatures on the Earth. Dinosaurs ruled the land, huge sea reptiles (plesiosaurs and ichthyosaurs) and giant turtles ruled the oceans, and flying reptiles (pterosaurs) dominated the air. Then, over a relatively short period of geological time, around 65 million years ago, most of these reptiles, including all the dinosaurs, disappeared. Mammals began to take over as the dominant life forms. No-one knows exactly what killed the dinosaurs.

PARENTAL CARE
Reptiles usually make nests of plant material in damp places or dig holes in the soil in which to lay their eggs. Some reptiles guard their eggs until they hatch. Pythons coil around their eggs to keep them warm and speed

▲Young lizards and snakes use a special egg tooth on their snout to chisel a way out of the eggs. Once the animals have hatched, this tooth is shed.

▼Inside the egg, the reptile embryo lies in a water-filled sac, the amnion. Blood vessels from its belly spread over the yolk sac to absorb food. The allantois stores the embryo's liquid waste. Oxygen passes into the egg through tiny holes in the shell, and waste gases from the embryo pass out.

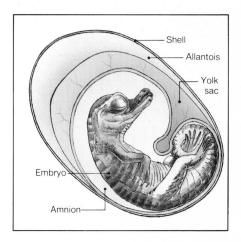

Shell

Allantois

Yolk sac

Embryo

Amnion

up hatching. The American alligator builds a nest of rotting vegetation. Heat from the decaying plants incubates the eggs.

Tortoises, crocodiles and geckos lay hard-shelled eggs, but most reptile eggs have soft, leathery shells. In many lizards and snakes the eggs develop inside the female, and the young are born alive.

COURTSHIP AND MATING

Most male reptiles display to attract a mate. Male lizards often have crests of skin on their heads or flaps of skin beneath their throats (dewlaps) which they can inflate to make themselves look bigger and more attractive to females, or more threatening to rival males. Dewlaps are often brightly colored. Male turtles bite the females to excite them, and courting snakes tickle each other with their scales prior to mating.

Reptiles have internal fertilization – the male has a tube-like organ to inject his sperm into the female. Thus they do not need to enter water to ensure that sperm reaches the eggs.

GROWING UP

From the moment they are born, most young reptiles are quite independent of their parents. Alligators may carry their young to nursery

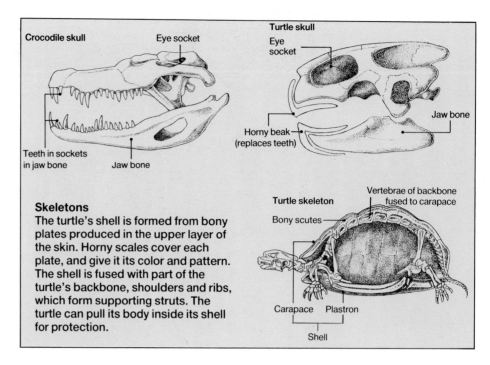

Skeletons
The turtle's shell is formed from bony plates produced in the upper layer of the skin. Horny scales cover each plate, and give it its color and pattern. The shell is fused with part of the turtle's backbone, shoulders and ribs, which form supporting struts. The turtle can pull its body inside its shell for protection.

pools and guard them for a time, but they do not feed them.

As a reptile grows, its scaly skin must also stretch. Most reptiles shed the outer, keratin-containing layer of the skin from time to time. A new layer of keratin forms underneath, then the old skin flakes or peels off. Reptiles with bony scales (scutes) add rings of new material to each scute as they grow. In snakes, skin-shedding may occur several times a year, being most frequent in young animals.

REPTILE FACTS
Heaviest Leatherback turtle, usually up to 1,500lb; record 1,903lb.
Smallest Gecko (lizard) *Sphaerodactylus parthenopion*, ¾in long.
Longest snake Reticulated python, 33ft long.
Largest lizard Komodo dragon, 350lb.
Largest crocodile Saltwater crocodile, 1,140 lb.
Largest dinosaur *Seismosaurus* ("earthshaker") from New Mexico, USA, was 118ft long and weighed 88 tons.
Longest lifespan Marion's tortoise, over 152 years.

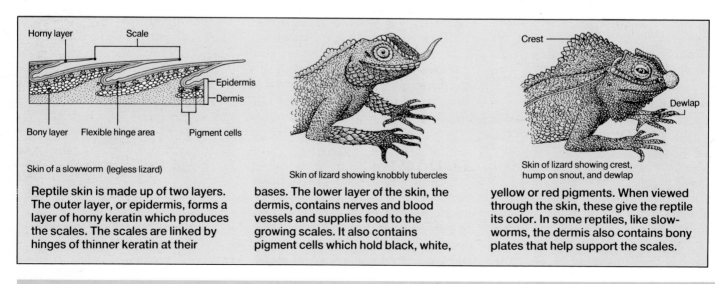

Skin of a slowworm (legless lizard)

Skin of lizard showing knobbly tubercles

Skin of lizard showing crest, hump on snout, and dewlap

Reptile skin is made up of two layers. The outer layer, or epidermis, forms a layer of horny keratin which produces the scales. The scales are linked by hinges of thinner keratin at their bases. The lower layer of the skin, the dermis, contains nerves and blood vessels and supplies food to the growing scales. It also contains pigment cells which hold black, white, yellow or red pigments. When viewed through the skin, these give the reptile its color. In some reptiles, like slowworms, the dermis also contains bony plates that help support the scales.

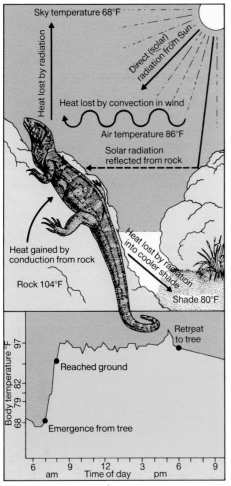

▲A chameleon lies in wait for a passing insect. This reptile can change its color to match its background – a perfect camouflage.

◁Heat flows from warm to cold objects. Reptiles use special behavior to control their body temperature. They are always losing heat to the air by radiation and convection. When they need to warm up to get active, they bask in the Sun, often on a hot rock. Here, they absorb heat from the Sun and from the rock. If they get too warm, they retreat to a shady place.

The graph shows how the lizard's body temperature is closely related to its behavior during the course of a day.

HUNTERS AND GRAZERS

Many tortoises and turtles, and some lizards, graze on plants. Most meat-eating reptiles rely on stealth and ambush to capture prey. They seize prey in their jaws. Many snakes have fangs which inject poison to paralyze or kill their prey or their enemies.

HOW REPTILES MOVE

Four-footed reptiles such as lizards and crocodiles are much more agile than amphibians. This is because their legs are placed almost under their bodies, so they can lift the body well clear of the ground. Despite this, the fastest reptile on land is a snake.

Snakes have several ways of moving. Usually they push the curves of the body against small bumps in the ground to thrust themselves forward. Some snakes can move in a straight line by using their scales as levers. Many snakes climb trees this way, hitching their scales into tiny ridges in the bark.

Lizards have claws on their feet, which help them to climb. Some curl their tail around twigs like an extra limb. Geckos have layers of microscopic projections armed with tiny bristles on their feet. These allow them to walk up smooth surfaces like glass window panes, and crawl upside down on the ceiling.

Crocodiles and lizards are good swimmers. Crocodiles swim like fish, wiggling through the water. The flattened tail is used as the main means of propulsion. Many turtles have flippers instead of legs, and can swim quite fast. The world's fastest reptile, at 20mph, is a swimming sea turtle.

SEA TURTLES

It is a moonlit night on a tropical island. On a sandy beach a huge black shape pulls itself out of the water. It heaves forward a few yards, then gives a huge sigh, and stops to rest. Slowly it moves above the tide mark and begins to dig. A female Green turtle has come ashore to lay her eggs. By dawn she will have gone back to sea.

All the warm oceans of the world contain sea turtles, and five of the seven species, including the Green turtle, are found around the world. Yet all species except one are in danger because of human activity.

SEA CHANGES

Compared with land tortoises, the sea turtles have a more lightweight shell. The bony part is reduced, but horny plates are still present on the outside, except in the Leatherback turtle. The shell is a streamlined shape. The legs have become flattened to form flippers. The front flippers are particularly long and the turtle flaps them up and down like wings to push itself through the water. In the sea, turtles can travel at speeds of over 18mph, although they usually move at a more leisurely pace of about 4mph.

Like all other reptiles, sea turtles breathe air with lungs. The length of time they can stay underwater depends on the species, the amount of oxygen in the water and how active the turtles are. If they are resting, it can be several weeks.

TURTLE TEARS

Sea turtles swallow seawater as they feed, and much of their food is also salty. To get rid of this extra salt, a sea turtle produces salty tears from a special gland close to each eye. The tears are produced all the time. In the sea the tears wash away, but on land a sea turtle always looks as if it is crying. The sea turtles' eyes are suited to see well in water, but in the air turtles are short-sighted.

BEACH NESTS

Sea turtles spend almost their entire lives in the water. But the pregnant females have to come on to the land to lay their eggs.

A female turtle lays her eggs in a hole on a sandy beach. She uses her back feet to scoop out a nest chamber, which must not get wet with salty water if the eggs are to develop. Turtle eggs are round, with shells like paper, and clutches of 60 to 150 are usual. A female Green turtle can lay 100 or more eggs at a time and may lay 11 clutches in one season, which lasts about 4 months. After laying a clutch,

◀A Green turtle swims through the sea above a coral reef. Clumsy on land, it moves gracefully when supported by water.

◄Hatchling Flatback turtles dash for the water. Birds catch many hatchlings before they reach the sea.

▼Species of turtle The Leatherback turtle (1) has a leathery skin over its shell, not horny plates. It feeds on jellyfish, some fish and crustaceans. The Green turtle (2) is so called because of the color of its fat. Adults feed near the shore on sea grasses.

the mother covers the eggs with sand and then drags herself back to the water. All this activity takes place in a single night, and is a great effort for an animal not built for moving on land.

HATCHING AS A GROUP

Turtle eggs need at least a month to develop, but hatch fastest when they are warm. The whole batch hatches together, and the baby turtles scurry instinctively to the bright light shining off the sea. A hatchling sea turtle weighs less than 1 ounce, but it may grow into an adult weighing 400lb.

LONG-DISTANCE TRAVELERS

In some turtle species, although they range widely in the sea, the number of important breeding sites is limited.

Green turtles in the southern Atlantic feed off the coast of South America, but travel 1,400 miles across the sea to Ascension Island to breed. The Atlantic ridley's breeding ground is on the Mexican coast. Here, 40,000 turtles may come ashore in just one night.

Although sea turtles produce many young, few survive to become adults. Some people hunt turtles for meat and for their shells. They also dig up and eat the eggs. In various locations, there are now projects to protect turtles and their breeding beaches. Eggs are dug up and incubated in safe places. When the hatchlings can fend for themselves, they are released.

TURTLES AND TERRAPINS

On a mudbank in a slow tropical river dozens of turtles bask in the Sun. Some turtles walk over the others as if they were part of the ground. The shadow of a large bird passes over them. Many turtles plunge into the water. With frantically paddling limbs they dive to the river bottom. Later, when all is quiet, their heads reappear one by one.

Of the 244 species of tortoise-like animals (chelonians) nearly 200 live in and around fresh water. At first sight an animal with a shell seems an unlikely design for the water, but it works well for a whole range of freshwater turtles. In most species the shell has become flatter and lighter compared with that of a land tortoise. It is also a more streamlined shape for swimming. Some turtles have no outer horny plates and the bony part of the shell has large spaces inside it.

These so-called softshell turtles have very flat shells which allow them to hide in the mud at the bottom of the water.

In many freshwater turtles the limbs are flattened and paddle-like. This is usually most obvious in types that rarely leave the water, but some pond tortoises that spend most of their time in water still have rounded limbs just like their land cousins.

BREATHING IN A BOX

The turtle's ribs make up part of the bony box of the shell. A turtle cannot move its ribs in and out to pump air in and out of its lungs as we can. Instead, muscles above the tops of the legs and in the abdomen provide the pumping action. Many aquatic turtles have extra ways of getting the oxygen they need. They may take in oxygen through their skin. The thin lining of the throat, or even special thin-walled sacs in the cloaca (the single posterior opening of the body), can also act as a kind of gill (an underwater breathing

structure). In well-oxygenated water some turtles can remain underwater almost forever. Some species hibernate underwater for weeks without needing to surface to breathe.

FINDING A MATE

In many turtle species the sexes look similar, but some species have markings which distinguish males from females. In the Carolina box turtle, males have red eyes, while those of females are yellow. In some turtles the males are smaller than the females. There may be other clues, such as a longer, thicker tail, or an incurved underside to the shell, which show that a turtle is a male. But in most species it seems to be behavior, rather than appearance, that allows the sexes to recognize one another.

To attract females, males use a variety of means, from biting and butting with the head, to special ways of swimming and stroking the female with their claws. In some turtles, such as the slider, where the male is much

---

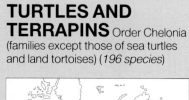

TURTLES AND TERRAPINS Order Chelonia (families except those of sea turtles and land tortoises) (*196 species*)

○ ■◻ ✦

▦ Habitat: rivers, lakes, swamps, estuaries; a few always on land.

◩ Diet: mainly meat, including insects, crustaceans, fish, molluscs, other animals; some species partly or wholly plant-eating.

○ Breeding: lay eggs. Depending on species: round or long, soft or brittle-shelled, clutch from 1-100.

Size: smallest (Bog turtle): 4½in long; longest (softshell turtles): up to 3½ft long; heaviest (Alligator snapping turtle): weight 200lb or more.

Color: mostly drab – brown, olive, gray; some have brightly colored markings.

Species mentioned in text:
Alligator snapping turtle (*Macroclemys temmincki*)
Australian snake-necked turtle (*Emydura macquarii*)
Bog turtle (*Clemmys muhlenbergii*)
Carolina box turtle (*Terrapene carolina*)
Florida redbelly turtle (*Pseudemys nelsonii*)
Giant snake-necked turtle (*Chelodina expansa*)
Matamata (*Chelus fimbriatus*)
Slider or Red-eared turtle (*Pseudemys scripta*)

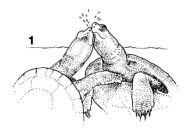

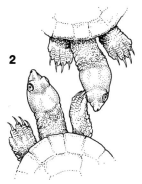

▲A male Australian snake-necked turtle courts a female by nudging her head above water (**1**), and by stroking her with his foot (**2**).

▲ ▼ **Species of turtle** This Spiny soft-shell turtle (*Trionyx spiniferus*) **(1)** of North America is "snorkeling." The male Red-eared turtle or slider **(2)** courts a female by fluttering his claws in front of her face. The New Guinea plateless turtle (*Carrettochelys insculpta*) **(3)** is a strong swimmer. The Musk turtle (*Staurotypus salvinii*) **(4)** comes from Central America. Skin flaps and flattened shape camouflage the matamata **(5)** of South America.

▲ ▼ **More species of turtle A** Yellow-spotted Amazon turtle (*Podocnemis unifilis*) **(1)** takes a breath at the surface. The Yellow mud turtle (*Kinosternon flavescens*) **(2)** digs a special burrow to lay its eggs. The adult Central American river turtle (*Dermatemys mawei*) **(3)**. The Big-headed turtle (*Platysternon megacephalum*) **(4)** is a good climber.

smaller than the female, the male has long claws on his front feet to help in his courtship dance. The male swims backwards in front of the female and fans her with his long claws.

EGG-LAYING

All freshwater turtles lay eggs on land, even if they spend the rest of their lives in the water. Species that live in places where conditions are the same throughout the year may breed at any time. But most turtles breed only at certain times of the year, such as in the early summer in cooler climates, or in time with either the wet or the dry season in the tropics.

Eggs are buried in the ground, or, in species such as the stinkpots, under decaying vegetation. As one might expect, the bigger species of turtle lay bigger eggs. The biggest freshwater turtles, with shell lengths of 32in, lay eggs 3in long – about the size of a medium-sized hen's egg.

Apart from choosing a suitable nest, turtles do not look after their eggs or young. The eggs are incubated by warmth from the Sun or rotting vegetation. The warmer the eggs are, the sooner they are likely to hatch. The eggs of some kinds of turtle do not develop right away so there may be a year between laying and hatching. The shortest time for development is about 2 months. In some species, the temperature during incubation is known to have an effect on the sex of the hatchlings. When temperatures are high more females are produced, and when temperatures are low more males are produced.

HATCHING AT THE RIGHT TIME
The baby turtle has a peg, or "egg-tooth," on the front of its snout, which helps it to escape from the egg. The egg-tooth drops off soon after hatching. The baby turtle hatches with a supply of yolk still in its body, and may not need to feed for some time.

Once they hatch, the babies do not always leave the nest straight away. In the northern USA, some snapping turtles overwinter in their nests as babies. Some Central American sliders have to wait for rain to soften the ground before they can escape from their nests. The longest waiting time on record was for some baby Giant snake-necked turtles in Australia that had to stay in their nest for 664 days until a drought ended.

GETTING WARM
An important part of the day for many turtles is the time they spend basking in the Sun. They come out of the water on to logs or sandbanks, spread their legs, and sunbathe. This helps warm their bodies to a good working temperature, and may also help digestion.

Mid-morning and late afternoon are the main basking times.

Good basking sites may be used by many turtles at the same time. Rich sources of food can also attract a crowd of turtles. But although these animals may sometimes congregate in large numbers, they do not form family or other social groups with any structure. Most turtles seem little interested in one another except as possible mates or rivals. One exception is the cleaning behavior seen in young sliders. They take it in turns to pull algae from one another's shells.

FEEDING METHODS
Most turtles feed on slow-moving prey, such as shellfish, worms and insect larvae. Many turtles eat some plants too. Diet may change with age. Baby sliders eat insects and other small animals, but adults have much more vegetable matter in their diet. Many turtles eat whatever plant or animal food they can find.

Some turtles have special ways of catching food. Snapping turtles have long bumpy necks and mud-colored skins. The shell is often covered in

▲ The strong high shell of the Florida redbelly turtle is unlike that of most aquatic species. It is a good defense against the crushing jaws of alligators.

algae. This helps the animals to lie hidden. They suddenly strike out with their powerful jaws at fish or smaller turtles. The matamata has very weak jaws. It catches its prey by opening its mouth wide. Water rushes into its mouth, taking the victim with it.

TOO SLOW AND DEFENSELESS
Populations of many river turtles and terrapins are declining today. Most seriously affected are the large river turtles and species with attractive shells. The main causes are destruction of their habitats, local killing for meat, and the demand from developed countries for luxury items such as turtle shell jewelry, leather goods and pets.

Unfortunately, the turtles' lumbering habits, their predictable nesting behavior and their passive actions when threatened make them highly susceptible to hunting by people at all times.

TORTOISES

A Gopher tortoise plods across a parched landscape, far from water. It moves to a cactus bush and reaches up to take a bite. It crushes a juicy cactus pad in its jaws, then rests a while in the shade. Eventually it moves off again to search for food, walking only 300ft in the next hour. For 50 years it has lived at this slow pace.

Land tortoises such as the Gopher are found on all the continents except Australia and Antarctica. Most inhabit the tropical regions of Africa, South America and Asia. They are related to the sea turtles (see pages 36-37) and the freshwater turtles and terrapins (pages 38-41).

ARMOR-PLATED
The most obvious feature of a tortoise is its shell. The inner part of the shell is bone. It is made from the backbone, ribs, and bony plates which are fused together in a solid box. The part which goes over the top of the tortoise is called the carapace and the part which goes beneath it is called the plastron. On the outside of the carapace and plastron are the horny plates that we see. These are equivalent to the scales on the body of other reptiles. The plates help to make the shell strong.

The hips and shoulders of a tortoise are inside the shell, which means they are inside the ribs – a very odd position compared with other back-boned animals. Many land tortoises can pull the head and legs within the shell for protection.

TORTOISES Testudinidae
(41 species)

Breeding: lay eggs, round or elongated. Clutches 1-50, depending on species.

Size: smallest (Madagascan spider tortoise): 4in long; largest (Aldabra giant tortoise): 4½ft long, weight 560lb.

Color: brown, greenish, yellow or black; sometimes patterned with rays or rings.

Species mentioned in text:
Aldabra or Indian Ocean giant tortoise
  (*Geochelone gigantea*)
Galapagos giant tortoise
  (*G. elephantopus*)
Gopher tortoise (*Gopherus polyphemus*)
Indian star tortoise (*Geochelone elegans*)
Madagascan spider tortoise (*Pyxis arachnoides*)
Radiated tortoise (*Geochelone radiata*)
Spur-thighed tortoise (*Testudo graeca*)

Habitat: land-living in warm areas of the world.

Diet: mostly plant-eating, some eat small animals.

PLANT-CRUSHERS

If you move slowly, you stand little chance of eating things that can run away. This may be why most land tortoises eat plants, unlike their water-living relatives which mainly eat meat. Tortoises do not possess teeth, just horny rims to the jaws. With these they bite, chop and crush plants until pieces are small enough to swallow.

Because tortoises move so slowly, they use up little energy and so are better than most reptiles at surviving long periods without food or drink. Giant tortoises can store some water in their bodies.

LONG LIFE

Tortoises live for longer than most other animals. Ages of well over 100 years have been proved for some tortoises, and their possible lifespan may be up to 200 years. The "record holder" is an Indian Ocean giant tortoise which was obtained as an

SLOW MOVERS

The strong shell of a land tortoise provides a good defense against many enemies, but its disadvantage is that it is heavy. Tortoises need strong thick legs to support their weight, and they are generally slow-moving. Charles Darwin watched a Galapagos tortoise that travelled at a rate of 4 miles per day. Most tortoises seem to move at less than ⅓ mile per hour. Much of the time they do not move at all.

◀Galapagos tortoises wallow in a pool. This behavior helps them to keep cool in hot weather.

▶Gopher tortoises mating. During courtship, the male Gopher tortoise bobs his head up and down and bites the female's shell and legs.

adult from the Seychelles Islands in 1766 and taken to Mauritius. It lived on Mauritius for 152 years until its death in 1918. It may have been up to 180 years old, but we can only guess at its true age.

A more doubtful record is for a Radiated tortoise, which died in 1966. This was supposed to have been given to the King of Tonga by Captain Cook at least 189 years earlier. Small tortoises can also be long-lived. One pet Spur-thighed tortoise has lived for 115 years. Tortoises carry a record of their age on their shells in the growth rings on the horny plates. In winter or in dry seasons they grow more slowly and this leaves a narrower ring. Counting the rings gives an estimate of a tortoise's age. It is not entirely reliable, as the oldest parts of the horny plate are often worn off.

ISLAND GIANTS

Most adult tortoises are at least 6in long, but a few species grow to over 24in long. The biggest tortoises live on the island of Aldabra, and nearby islands in the Indian Ocean, and on the Galapagos Islands in the Pacific. These giant tortoises can have a shell length of 3ft or more. Before people visited the islands, these tortoises were the biggest land animals there. With less need for protection their shells became relatively light, but they are still massive animals. Weights of 330lb are common.

Young giant tortoises can grow fast in good conditions. One grew from a weight of 28lb to 360lb in just 7 years. Older tortoises may still grow, but at a slower rate.

SAVE THE TORTOISES

Early seafarers who discovered the Galapagos and Aldabra Islands soon found that the tortoises were easily caught as a source of meat. They killed many to eat on the spot. They also loaded thousands of tortoises into their ships, and killed them when they needed fresh meat. It is not surprising that the numbers of tortoises were greatly reduced and they disappeared altogether from some islands. On the Galapagos Islands, settlers and their tame animals, such as goats and dogs, (which were allowed to run wild or escaped) also affected tortoise populations. Now attempts are being made to breed giant tortoises in captivity to keep up their numbers.

HISTORY OF THE GIANTS

How did the giant tortoises get to the Galapagos Islands? This is a question which has fascinated many people. It is almost certain that the ancestors of these tortoises came from South America, which even today has some quite large species. Ocean currents run from the South American mainland past the Galapagos Islands. Tortoises could have been carried on a raft of vegetation to the Galapagos.

Once on the Galapagos Islands, the tortoises bred and adapted to their new surroundings. In the process they became very big. They also developed into different types on the various islands of the group. (The types could inter-breed and so still belonged to the same species.) Some types had rounded shells; others had longer, flatter shells. One type even developed a high front to the shell (saddleback). The length of the neck also became different in different types. Long-necked, saddleback tortoises, for example, were adapted to lift their heads high to browse on shrubs.

When Charles Darwin was traveling round the world from 1831 to 1836 he visited the Galapagos. He was impressed by the differences between the tortoises on different islands. They helped to give him his ideas about how evolution may have taken place.

▶A courting pair of Galapagos giant tortoises. The male is larger than the female. The survival of these giant reptiles is threatened by rats and pigs which eat tortoise eggs and young.

LIZARDS

It is a warm day. There is a movement in the heather. A tiny head appears, followed by a long body and an even longer tail. A European common lizard is hunting. It turns its head on one side, listening and watching the vegetation intently. Suddenly it pounces, and snaps up a small spider.

Lizards are found on all continents except Antarctica. Most lizards are found in the tropics, but some live in cooler climates. The European common lizard lives as far north as the Arctic Circle in Scandinavia. There are 16 families of lizards. This article deals with the broad category of lizards. On pages 50-59 you can read about five of the most distinctive families, from chameleons to monitor lizards.

LIZARDS Sub-order Sauria
(3,751 species)

● ◧ ☠

◼ **Habitat:** all types of habitat from wet forest to desert; on all continents and many islands where temperature not too low.

■ **Diet:** usually small animals, but some are plant-eaters.

◎ **Breeding:** typically lay eggs after internal fertilization. Some give birth to live young.

Size: smallest (Virgin Islands gecko, see page 54): total length 1⅓in; largest (Komodo dragon): length 10ft, weight up to 350 lb.

Color: highly variable including green, brown, black and some bright colors.

Species mentioned in text:
Armadillo girdle-tailed lizard (*Cordylus cataphractus*)
Australian frilled lizard (*Chlamydosaurus kingii*)
European common lizard (*Lacerta vivipara*)
Flying dragon (*Draco volans*)
Komodo dragon (*Varanus komodoensis*).
Sharp-snouted snake lizard (*Lialis burtonis*)
Slow-worm (*Anguis fragilis*)
Sri Lanka prehensile-tail lizard (*Cophotis celanica*)
Sungazer (*Cordylus giganteus*)

◀▲ Species of lizard Granite night lizard (*Xantusia henshawi*) **(1)** of California. Sharp-snouted snake lizard **(2)** of Australia. Common tegu (*Tupinambis teguixin*) **(3)** of South America. Colorado checkered whiptail (*Cnemidophorus tesselatus*) **(4)**. Flat lizard (*Platysaurus intermedius*) **(5)** of South Africa. Ocellated lizard (*Lacerta lepida*) **(6)** of western Mediterranean area.

A TYPICAL LIZARD

As may be expected in a group with nearly 4,000 species, lizards come in many different shapes and sizes. But a typical lizard is a fairly small animal, perhaps 4 to 8in long; about half this length is the tail. A lizard has four legs, and its body is covered in small scales. It has good eyesight, and can see colors. The eyelids are usually movable. At the back of the head are small ear openings.

A lizard uses its tongue to help it "taste" the surroundings. It is a hunter, ambushing or hunting down small animals, often insects. To reproduce, a typical lizard lays eggs.

OVER AND UNDERGROUND

Some lizards have become especially good at climbing, and a few, such as the Sri Lanka prehensile-tail lizard, even use their tail to hold on to branches. The Flying dragons of Asia are small lizards that have taken to the air. They climb trees and then jump from one tree to another, gliding on "wings" of skin. The skin is stretched over very long ribs, which stick out from the sides of the body.

At the other extreme are lizards that live underground. Many of these lizards have either very small legs or no legs at all. Their eyes may be tiny or even beneath the skin. When the eyes still work, each may be covered by a transparent "spectacle" instead of eyelids. The "spectacle" helps to protect the eye from damage or injury.

Some lizards, such as the water dragons of the Far East, are good swimmers. Others, such as the Australian frilled lizard, are able to run fast on their hind legs for a short distance if they need to escape an enemy.

RITUAL FIGHTS

Most lizards live on their own, but some species do react to other lizards. A few lizards are territorial, and the males threaten any rivals which enter their territory. This may be done by rituals such as head-bobbing, rather than actual fighting. Lizards with this type of behavior are often brightly colored to increase the impact of the display. Colors may also be used to attract a mate.

DEFENSE AND ESCAPE
Lizards have many ways of protecting themselves from other animals that may eat them. They often keep very still, and their colors may allow them to blend into the surroundings. Some have specially tough scales. The plated lizards of Africa have bone underneath their scales. Other lizards have long spiny scales, which makes them difficult for an enemy to swallow. The sungazer will lash its spiny tail at an attacker. The Armadillo girdle-tailed lizard often simply wedges itself in a crevice for protection.

▼ **More species of lizard** The Southern alligator lizard (*Elgaria multicarinata*) (1) of America has strong limbs, but is related to the slow-worm. The Chinese xenosaur (*Shinisaurus crocodilurus*) (2) lives along streams. The sungazer (3) uses its spiny tail for defense. The Bornean earless lizard (*Lanthanotus borneensis*) (4) is a good swimmer. The Gila monster (*Heloderma suspectum*) (5) is venomous, with fangs in its bottom jaw. The Asian blind lizard (*Dibamus novaeguineae*) (6) lives underground. It has eyes under the skin.

◄The slow-worm is a European legless lizard that grows to about 18in long. It can live for more than 50 years.

Quite a different way of using the tail for defense is shown by wall lizards and slow-worms. By contracting some tail muscles, these lizards can make the tail break off at special weak areas in the tail bones. If it is attacked, the lizard drops its tail and leaves it behind, wriggling, as a decoy. The tail may continue to wriggle for several minutes. The lizard escapes; later it grows a replacement tail. Some lizards have specially colored tails that attract additional attention.

The greatest threats to such lizards, however, are not natural predators, but humans. Especially in sub-tropical regions, the lizards' habitats are being altered or destroyed such that their populations are unlikely to recover.

EGGS OR LIVE YOUNG?

Most lizards lay eggs. A clutch of about 20 is very common. But some lizards produce live young. In most of these live-bearers, the mother lizard keeps the eggs inside her body until they are ready to hatch. The yolk inside the egg nourishes the young in the usual way. In a few lizards, such as the night lizards, a placenta forms so the babies can obtain some nourishment from the mother.

Live-bearing may be useful in difficult conditions, such as in places where summers are cool. The European common lizard produces live young in the north of its range, but lays eggs in the south, where summers are warmer. Strangest of all are a few lizard species in which no males are known. Females are able to produce a new generation of "look-alike" lizards on their own.

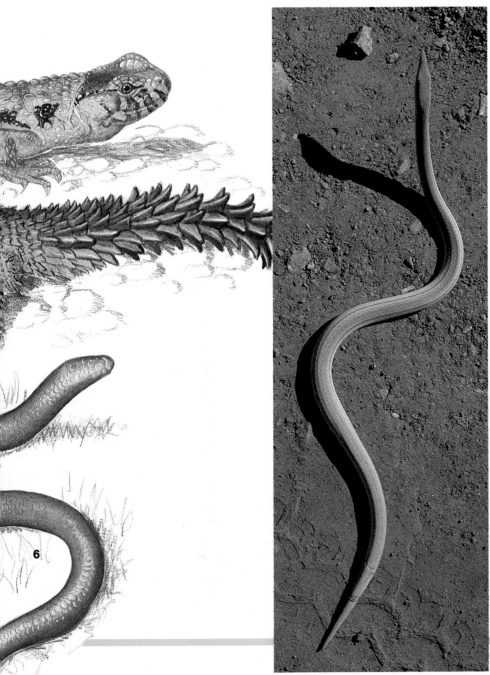

6

◄The Sharp-snouted snake lizard has no front limbs, and small flaps for hind limbs. It eats other lizards.

CHAMELEONS

A chameleon moves slowly along a twig. As it moves, its body rocks backwards and forwards like a leaf in the wind. It is watching a grasshopper on the next branch. It edges to within 6in of the unsuspecting insect. Suddenly, faster than the eye can follow, the chameleon's tongue shoots out and back, pulling the grass-hopper into its mouth.

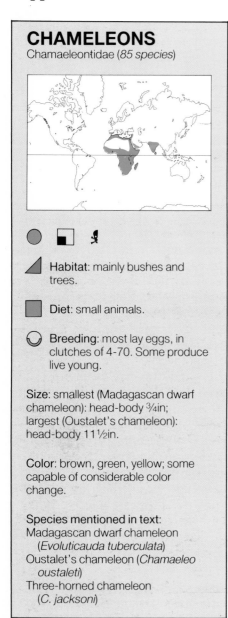

CHAMELEONS
Chamaeleontidae (*85 species*)

▲ **Habitat:** mainly bushes and trees.

■ **Diet:** small animals.

◗ **Breeding:** most lay eggs, in clutches of 4-70. Some produce live young.

Size: smallest (Madagascan dwarf chameleon): head-body ¾in; largest (Oustalet's chameleon): head-body 11½in.

Color: brown, green, yellow; some capable of considerable color change.

Species mentioned in text:
Madagascan dwarf chameleon (*Evoluticauda tuberculata*)
Oustalet's chameleon (*Chamaeleo oustaleti*)
Three-horned chameleon (*C. jacksoni*)

Nearly all species of chameleon live in forests in Africa and Madagascar, feeding mainly on insects. One species lives in southern Europe; another is found in southern Asia.

TREE-CLIMBING
Chameleons have many odd features not found in any other lizards. For example, a chameleon has long legs, but they bend at the knee and elbow so that the feet go under the body. To grip a branch, a chameleon puts two toes around one side and the other three toes round the other side. The sharp claws on its feet also help it to grip. Chameleons generally move slowly, and can hold on tightly with at least two feet at once. In addition, most chameleons have a useful pre-hensile tail, which can be coiled around twigs to act as an anchor.

ALL-SEEING EYES
The eyes of a chameleon are mounted on movable turrets. These can be turned in all directions. Like most lizards, chameleons can move one eye independently of the other. One eye may be looking forward and down, while the other eye looks backwards and up.

A chameleon can scan all round for danger or possible meals. Sometimes, though, it is useful to have both eyes working together. A chameleon can swivel its eyes so that both look forward to focus on the same object. This helps it to judge distances when it is climbing or hunting.

TERRIFIC TONGUE
A chameleon's diet consists mainly of insects and spiders. Some of the larger species eat small birds and mammals. These are rarely caught with the jaws in the usual lizard fashion. Instead, the chameleon relies on its special tongue. The tongue normally rests folded inside the mouth, but it can be squeezed by special muscles and cata-pulted out to catch prey.

The tongue is often longer than the chameleon's head and body, and it can be used to hit an insect some distance away. It can be shot out and pulled back in as little time as 0.04 seconds. Its swollen tip can grasp prey and is also sticky so the prey cannot escape as it is pulled into the mouth.

COLOR CHANGE
Chameleons are famous for their ability to change color. Most kinds are basically brown, green or yellowish, which helps to camouflage them in trees and bushes. But many species are able to change color and pattern by moving pigments in the skin. They can change from almost white to almost black, with many shades and variations on their "natural" color.

Colors may change completely in just a few minutes. The chameleon does not seem to be changing color to match the background color. The amount of light, the temperature, and the mood of the animal – whether it is angry or frightened for example – may have more effect. But the chameleon's

colors are often sufficiently like the surroundings to make the animal very difficult to see.

LONE LIZARDS

Chameleons prefer to be alone most of the time. They are territorial and males fight to keep other males out of their territory. Fights are somewhat slow-motion affairs, but they can be long and vicious. Horned species use their horns in combat.

During courtship, male chameleons also display aggressively. After mating, the female may not lay eggs immediately, as she can store sperm for long periods. A few species of pygmy chameleon give birth to live young. The newborn often stay surrounded by the transparent egg membrane for several hours.

◀When threatened, chameleons may inflate their bodies, hiss, and expose the bright skin which lines the mouth.

▼A Three-horned chameleon shooting out its tongue with deadly accuracy to take hold of a fly.

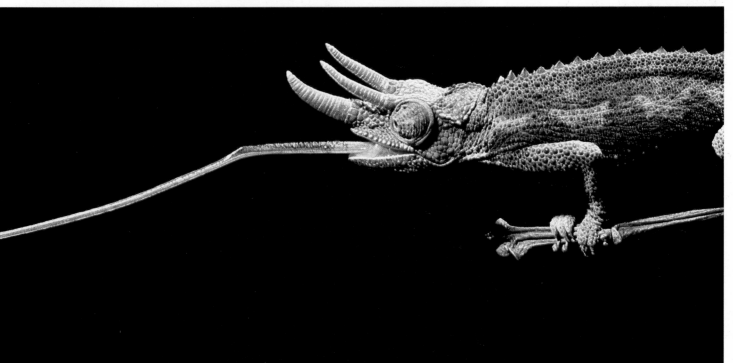

IGUANAS

On a bush at the edge of a Central American forest a competition is taking place between two tiny lizards. One spreads out a fan of red skin beneath its throat. The other replies with another flash of scarlet. They move around the bush, flicking their bright throat fans until one, intimidated by the display of his rival, scuttles away.

The iguana family of lizards is a large and diverse one, but most species have well-developed social systems in which such visual displays are important. Nearly all the iguanas live in the tropical regions of the Americas.

SWIMMERS AND RUNNERS
Some iguanas are climbers. These include the Green iguana of South American rain forests and the many species of anoles. A few of these climbers have a prehensile tail. Green iguanas, and several other species, are equally at home on land and in the water. They can swim well, or remain submerged for a long time.

Other iguanas live on the ground; many of them have a flattened body. Some of the ground-dwellers are fast runners, travelling at up to 15mph for short distances. The Desert iguana and the basilisk can run on their hind legs. A few iguanas are burrowers. Fringe-toed lizards have a fringe of scales on the toes which helps them to "swim" swiftly through sand. These lizards will dive into sand to escape danger. When they walk on the surface, the fringes help them to grip the sand.

BIZARRE ANT-EATER
Another burrower is the Horned toad which lives in the deserts of North

►Few lizards go in water, but the Marine iguana of the Galapagos swims in the sea to feed on seaweeds.

IGUANAS Iguanidae
(*650 species*)

Habitat: varied; ranges from rain forest to desert.

Diet: insects and other small animals; some kinds wholly or partly plant-eating.

Breeding: most lay eggs, clutches 1-45. Some produce live young.

Size: most 8-15in. Smallest (Texas tree-lizard): head-tail 4in; largest (Marine iguana): head-tail 53in.

Color: gray, black, brown; some green or other bright colors.

Species mentioned in text:
Basilisk (*Basiliscus basiliscus*)
Collared lizard (*Crotaphytus collaris*)
Desert iguana (*Dipsosaurus dorsalis*)
Fence lizard (*Sceloporus undulatus*)
Fringe-toed lizard (*Uma notata*)
Galapagos land iguana (*Conolophus subcristatus*)
Green iguana (*Iguana iguana*)
Horned toad (*Phrynosoma cornutum*)
Marine iguana (*Amblyrhynchus cristatus*)
Texas tree-lizard (*Urosaurus ornatus*)

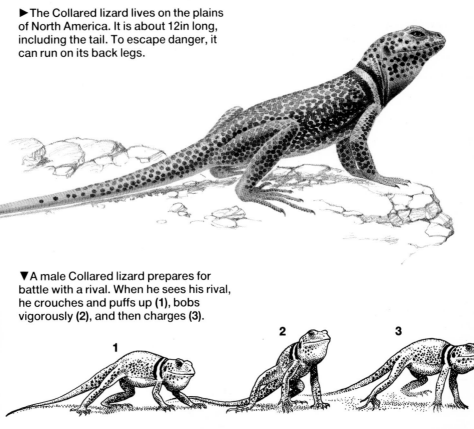

America. This lizard is covered with sharp spiny scales, which are especially large at the back of the head. It sometimes digs into sand so that just its eyes are showing. It preys on ants. When it is attacked by mammals or birds it may spray blood from its eyes.

Most of the smaller species of the iguana family eat insects or other small animals, but the bigger iguanas eat plant material. The Green iguana feeds on fruit, leaves and flowers, and the Galapagos land iguana will even eat cacti.

The Desert iguana of the western USA sometimes climbs up into creosote bushes to eat the flowers and leaves. This small lizard goes underground at night, often into a rodent burrow, to avoid the cold. In the daytime the temperature in the desert can be very high. The Desert iguana often has a body temperature of 104°F, and can be active, at least for a short while, when its temperature is 116°F. This temperature would kill most other animals.

SHOWING THE FLAG

Many male iguanas display to defend a territory from other males, or to attract females. In such species the males may be larger than the females, more brightly colored, or have extra adornments. In the Fence lizard, for example, the male has blue patches on his throat and belly. He bobs up and down with his whole body to display these and so warn other males to keep away. When he is courting a female he bobs with just his head and front legs. Females also use signals. A female unwilling to mate will lift her whole body stiffly off the ground to discourage the male.

EGGS AND NESTS

Some anoles lay just a single egg in a clutch, but they may lay more clutches at 2-week intervals. A Green iguana may lay 20 or more eggs, but several females may choose the same spot to lay, so the number of eggs in a nest may be higher than this.

IGUANAS AND PEOPLE

Large iguanas, such as the Green iguana, are meaty and some people find them good to eat. Iguana eggs are also a popular food. The eggs have a large yolk. In some places, this has had a bad effect on lizard numbers. In the West Indies, a more difficult problem are the animals, such as cats and mongooses, which have been introduced by people. These animals eat the iguanas and their eggs. Some species are now greatly endangered. In some cases, all the young have been destroyed, leaving only adults which are probably too old to breed.

▶The Collared lizard lives on the plains of North America. It is about 12in long, including the tail. To escape danger, it can run on its back legs.

▼A male Collared lizard prepares for battle with a rival. When he sees his rival, he crouches and puffs up (1), bobs vigorously (2), and then charges (3).

GECKOS

As night falls in a town in the tropics, the people turn on the lights. From its hiding place behind a picture on a wall, a small lizard emerges. It runs up the wall and across the ceiling, close to a lamp that is attracting insects. It snaps up several insects, ignoring the people preparing a meal below. They are pleased to see the gecko at work above them, removing pests from the house.

Geckos are probably best known for their ability to climb on almost any surface, from bark to walls, ceilings and even sheet glass. They live over most of the warmer parts of the world and are common in the tropics. Some species are found on islands far out in the oceans.

EGG TRAVELERS
Geckos have spread where other lizards could not, probably because of the way they lay their eggs. There are usually two eggs which are stuck underneath tree bark. The eggs have tough shells, and may take several months to develop. During this time storms may wash a log out to sea and the ocean currents may carry it to another island. If the eggs survive the journey and hatch on the new land, the baby geckos may start a colony.

NIGHT NOISES
Geckos are unusual among reptiles in that they have a voice, not just a hiss. Most are nocturnal, and have good hearing, so noises are a good way of communicating. They make chirping, clicking or barking noises and have different combinations of sounds for courting or defending a territory.

▶The Tokay gecko of South-east Asia is one of the noisiest geckos. It can make a barking sound as loud as a dog.

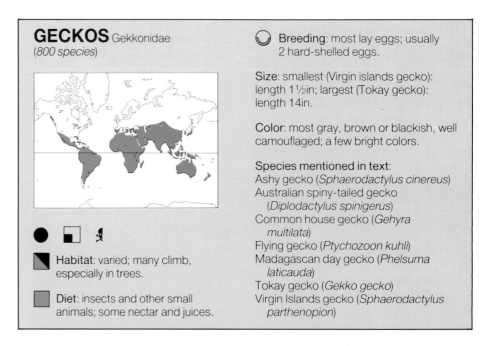

GECKOS Gekkonidae
(*800 species*)

● ▣ 𝕬

◣ Habitat: varied; many climb, especially in trees.

▢ Diet: insects and other small animals; some nectar and juices.

◡ Breeding: most lay eggs; usually 2 hard-shelled eggs.

Size: smallest (Virgin islands gecko): length 1½in; largest (Tokay gecko): length 14in.

Color: most gray, brown or blackish, well camouflaged; a few bright colors.

Species mentioned in text:
Ashy gecko (*Sphaerodactylus cinereus*)
Australian spiny-tailed gecko (*Diplodactylus spinigerus*)
Common house gecko (*Gehyra multilata*)
Flying gecko (*Ptychozoon kuhli*)
Madagascan day gecko (*Phelsuma laticauda*)
Tokay gecko (*Gekko gecko*)
Virgin Islands gecko (*Sphaerodactylus parthenopion*)

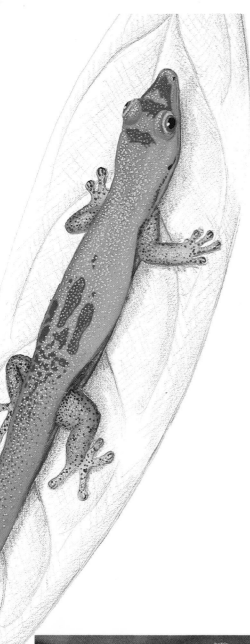

WEARING SPECTACLES

Instead of having the usual lizard eyelids, nearly all geckos have a large transparent "spectacle" over each eye. They are unable to clean this protective covering by blinking, but many put their tongue out and use it to wipe their eyes.

The pupil of the eye can open very wide, which helps the gecko to see in the dark. In sunlight, the pupil is closed to a slit with a few little chinks in it. These let in enough light for the gecko's sensitive eyes to work well in the daytime.

DEFENSE TACTICS

The tails of geckos vary. Some species have ordinary tapering tails, others have tails that are flattened or shaped like leaves or turnips. All geckos can readily drop their tail if they are attacked. Some geckos, such as the Common house gecko, will also shed large portions of skin if they are picked up. Another method of escape is used by the Flying gecko. This gecko has flaps of skin along its body and tail, which allow it to glide from one tree to another to avoid danger.

One of the strangest means of defense is used by the Australian spiny-tailed geckos. Instead of losing their tails, these geckos can shoot out sticky, strong-smelling threads from special pits in the tail. These threads can travel up to 12in and trap a predator in a "cobweb."

CLINGING CLIMBERS

Most geckos have sharp claws and clinging toes, but the interesting part of a gecko's foot is underneath the toes. Here there are many ridges of scales. On these scales are millions of tiny "hairs," which can only be seen under a microscope. The hairs help the geckos to grip the tiny bumps and dips in a surface, even when it appears to be completely smooth. Some tree geckos have prehensile tails, and these too may have microscopic "hairs" underneath them. The animals use their tails to grasp twigs.

◄This male Madagascan day gecko is more colorful than the female which has a drab brownish skin.

►The camouflage pattern of the Australian spiny-tailed gecko usually hides it against tree bark. It is spreading its toes well to get a grip.

▼An Ashy gecko sheds its skin as part of the growth process. This lizard is found in Florida and the Caribbean.

SKINKS

Under a rotting log is a nest of 15 small eggs. A female Five-lined skink returns to this nest and touches each egg in turn with her tongue. She turns some with her snout and moves others slightly. For a while she rests. In one of the eggs movement can be seen, and a slit has begun to appear in the shell. Her babies are about to hatch.

Several skink species, such as the Five-lined, are unusual among reptiles in that they display parental care. Skinks are the most numerous lizards and are found throughout the tropics and the warmer temperate regions, including many islands out in the oceans. They live in many different habitats, from deserts to forests. They may live on the ground, in trees, or below the ground.

Yet in some ways the skink family is not so varied as some of the smaller lizard families. Most species have a rather pointed head, a long body, short legs and a long tapered tail.

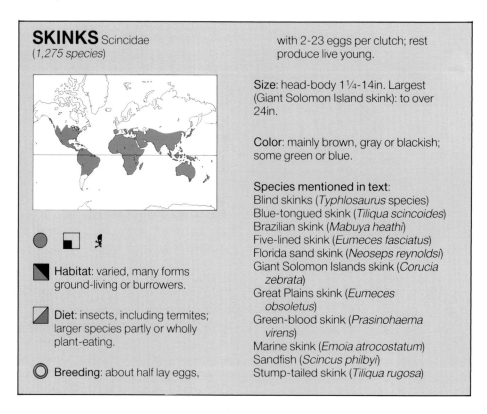

SKINKS Scincidae
(*1,275 species*)

Habitat: varied, many forms ground-living or burrowers.

Diet: insects, including termites; larger species partly or wholly plant-eating.

Breeding: about half lay eggs, with 2-23 eggs per clutch; rest produce live young.

Size: head-body 1¼-14in. Largest (Giant Solomon Island skink): to over 24in.

Color: mainly brown, gray or blackish; some green or blue.

Species mentioned in text:
Blind skinks (*Typhlosaurus* species)
Blue-tongued skink (*Tiliqua scincoides*)
Brazilian skink (*Mabuya heathi*)
Five-lined skink (*Eumeces fasciatus*)
Florida sand skink (*Neoseps reynoldsi*)
Giant Solomon Islands skink (*Corucia zebrata*)
Great Plains skink (*Eumeces obsoletus*)
Green-blood skink (*Prasinohaema virens*)
Marine skink (*Emoia atrocostatum*)
Sandfish (*Scincus philbyi*)
Stump-tailed skink (*Tiliqua rugosa*)

▲The sandfish lives in deserts. It "swims" swiftly through the sand just below the surface, hunting for beetles.

OUT OF SIGHT

Some of those skinks that climb have glands on their feet which may stop them falling from trees. Only the giant of the family, the Giant Solomon Islands skink, has a tail developed for holding on. Many species live among the debris and leaf litter lying on the ground, and others burrow. Burrowers move by wriggling the body from side-to-side to push themselves along. They are mostly small and secretive animals, and quickly "swim" downwards through the sand when they are approached.

In the skink family some species have legs of normal proportions while others have tiny legs or no legs at all. The number of toes also varies between species. Some have five toes; others have no toes at all. Several or all toes may bear tiny fringes. The Florida sand skink has a single toe on each front foot and two on the rear feet. Its hind legs are twice the size of the front legs. These seem to be adaptations to the animal's burrowing life-style.

EYES AND EARS

Other parts of the body that are often reduced for life underground are the eyes. In many burrowing skinks the lower eyelids have become thickened to protect the eyes and are more or less fixed in place. A "window" in these eyelids allows the skinks to look out. The blind skinks of South Africa have eyes that are completely covered by scales. In all these species, the ear openings are also very small or closed up altogether. The animals can hear through the bones of their head, which vibrate in step with external sound waves.

ADVANCED BREEDING

Several skink species show unusual breeding behavior for reptiles. Some egg-laying species, such as Five-lined skinks, stay near their eggs and look after them. Great Plains skink mothers have even been seen licking their babies clean after they hatch. In some species, the babies may stay close to the mother for a while after hatching.

Among the live-bearers are species, such as the Brazilian skink, in which the young are nourished by their mother through a placenta, in very much the same way as a mammal. Most live-bearers have fewer young than egg-layers. The Blue-tongued skink, for example, has about ten young. The Stump-tailed skink has only two young, but each one is almost half as long as its mother.

▼A Blue-tongued skink displays the tongue from which it gets its name. This display is used to frighten enemies.

UNUSUAL SPECIES
The Green-blood skink lives in the trees. It is green above and yellow below. Unlike all other animals with backbones, it has green blood. The green coloring of the blood even makes the tongue and mouth lining green. When the lizard gapes, its green mouth can be clearly seen. Its eggs are also green. They are laid among the foliage, well hidden from predators.

The Stump-tailed skink from Australia has a fat triangular tail that looks like a head. The animal stores fat in the tail. It is difficult to tell which way the

skink is going and this may help to confuse enemies. This species feeds on slow-moving prey such as snails, plus fruits and other plant material. In fact, many other large skinks, such as the Blue-tongued skink, eat plants.

One of the most unusual life-styles is that of the Marine skink of the Bismarck Archipelago. This species catches crabs on the beach and sometimes swims in the sea to find food or to keep cool. It is an excellent swimmer, and will readily take to water if threatened. It can remain submerged for several minutes.

MONITORS

A monitor lizard appears on the river bank. It is searching for food. Halfway down the sandy bank, it pauses and tests the ground with its tongue. Then it starts to scratch away the sand with its claws. It puts its head into the hole, lifts out an egg and swallows. It has found a crocodile's nest. It feeds greedily and quickly, before the owner returns.

Monitor lizards comprise a small family of rather large lizards. They live in Africa, southern Asia and the East Indies, and particularly in the Australian region, where 24 of the 31 species are found. As well as feeding on eggs, monitors eat carrion and a wide variety of adult animals.

Monitor lizards have long necks and a relatively short body. The head is rather long and narrow, with a pointed snout. The slit-like nostrils are often near the eyes. The teeth are sharp and fang-like. In all species, the legs are strong, with five strong toes each armed with sharp claws. The tail is not fragile, as in some lizards, but is long and muscular. It is sometimes used as a weapon.

ACTIVE KILLERS
Monitors are active in the day, when most species search for food. All monitors are meat-eaters. The smaller kinds live mainly on grasshoppers, beetles and other insects, but many monitors catch other reptiles, or birds and mammals, as well. The Komodo dragon, the biggest living lizard, has been known to overcome a 1,300lb adult Water buffalo.

Monitors tend to swallow their prey whole, or in huge chunks. They also have large appetites. A 100lb Komodo dragon once ate in one meal a whole wild pig that weighed 90lb. This species of monitor has been recorded as attacking and killing people.

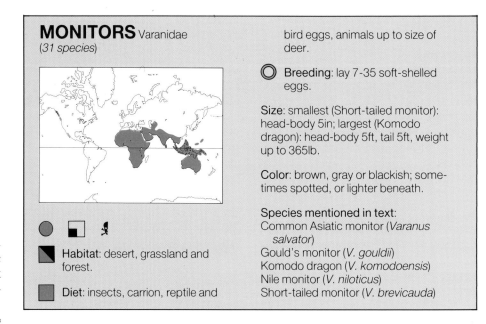

MONITORS Varanidae
(*31 species*)

● ◐ ☠

■ **Habitat:** desert, grassland and forest.

■ **Diet:** insects, carrion, reptile and bird eggs, animals up to size of deer.

◎ **Breeding:** lay 7-35 soft-shelled eggs.

Size: smallest (Short-tailed monitor): head-body 5in; largest (Komodo dragon): head-body 5ft, tail 5ft, weight up to 365lb.

Color: brown, gray or blackish; sometimes spotted, or lighter beneath.

Species mentioned in text:
Common Asiatic monitor (*Varanus salvator*)
Gould's monitor (*V. gouldii*)
Komodo dragon (*V. komodoensis*)
Nile monitor (*V. niloticus*)
Short-tailed monitor (*V. brevicauda*)

▲ In courtship, a male Komodo dragon presses his snout against the female **(1)**, tests her with his tongue, scratches her back **(2)**, and then mates **(3)**.

▼ This Common Asiatic monitor shows the typical strong claws of monitors, and the long, forked tongue, which constantly tests the surroundings.

◀Komodo dragons prey on animals as large as deer or wild pigs. They are agile, and swim and climb well.

▼Gould's monitor lives in the deserts of Australia. When threatened by an enemy, it rears up on its back legs.

ALERT AND LIVELY

Many monitors hold their heads erect on their long necks, which makes them look especially alert. Most live on the ground, and some are good climbers and swimmers.

Water monitors are able to catch fish. The Common Asiatic monitor can stay underwater for an hour; it often takes to the water to avoid enemies. It has even been seen swimming far out at sea. It moves through the water by flapping its tail from side to side; the legs are kept motionless close to the body. Several species are able to run fast. Gould's monitor can run faster than a person over a short distance.

SELF-DEFENSE

If threatened, monitor lizards can put on a frightening performance. They hiss loudly, puff their throats out, turn sideways and may rear up to make themselves look as large as possible. They also lash out with the tail, which can give a very hard blow. Finally, if necessary, they will scratch and bite fiercely.

EATEN BY AN ALLY

In the breeding season, fights take place between the males. Monitors lay eggs in holes in river banks or in trees along the edge of rivers or streams. The Nile monitor often lays its eggs in termite nests. As in most reptiles, monitors do not protect their young. Eggs may even be dug up and eaten by other monitors.

SNAKES

In the reeds at the water's edge a Water snake waits. It is partly coiled and lies still. Only the occasional flick of the tongue shows that this snake is alert. A frog hops from the water. Stealthily the snake glides forward, so smoothly that the frog doesn't notice. Then the snake strikes. It seizes the frog in its jaws, and begins to swallow it whole.

Snakes are a large and successful group. They occur on all continents except Antarctica and are found in all regions except the very coldest ones. water snakes, for example, range from Scandinavia to northern Australia. Snakes have even reached many isolated islands, although they do not live on some islands such as Ireland.

SNAKES OF MANY TYPES

About two-thirds of all snake species belong to the large family Colubridae, which includes familiar species such as the European grass snake and the North American garter snakes. Most members of this family are harmless to humans; a few species have poison fangs at the back of the mouth.

SNAKES Sub-order Serpentes
(2,389 species)

Habitat: most ground-living, but many burrow, climb trees, or live in fresh or sea water.

Diet: other animals, from slugs and insects to mammals, fish, other reptiles, birds and eggs.

Breeding: internal fertilization, usually followed by egg-laying. Many species bear live young.

Size: most 10-60in. Shortest (West Indian thread snake): 5in; longest (Reticulated python, see p.64): 33ft.

Color: mostly brown, gray or black. Some bright colors or vivid markings.

Species mentioned in text:
African egg-eating snake (*Dasypeltis scaber*)
Boomslang (*Dispholidus typus*)
Costa Rican parrot snake (*Leptophis depressirostris*)
European grass snake (*Natrix natrix*)
Flowerpot snake (*Rhamphotyphlops braminus*)
Milk snake (*Lampropeltis triangulum*)
Redbelly snake (*Storeria occipitomaculata*)
Toad-eater snake (*Xenodon rabdocephalus*)
West Indian thread snake (*Leptotyphlops bilineata*)

▼**Snake species of several families** Texas blind snake (*Leptotyphlops dulcis*) (1). Shieldtail snake (*Uropeltis ocellatus*) (2). Montpellier snake (*Malpolon monspessulanus*) (3). Cuban Island ground boa (*Tropidophis melanurus*) (4). Malaysian pipe snake (*Cylindrophis rufus*) (5). Schlegel's blind snake (*Typhlops schlegeli*) (6).

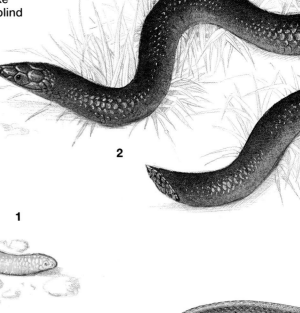

1

2

Other types of snake include the primitive pythons and boas (see pages 64-67), the very poisonous cobras and sea-snakes (pages 68-73) and the vipers and rattlesnakes (pages 74-77).

PIPES AND THREADS

There are also six families of rather odd, mainly small, burrowing snakes, which contain 338 known species.

The 11 species of pipesnake live in the tropical areas of South America and Asia. They are all less than 3ft long and burrow in damp soil. They feed on other snakes and eels. To fool enemies, many pipesnakes hide their head and wave the tail, which is red underneath.

The thread snakes number 78 species and include some of the smallest snakes; several are less than 20cm in length and no thicker than a matchstick. They live in tropical rain forests and feed on ants and termites.

FEMALE TRAVELER

The blind snakes live in the tropics. Their eyes are tiny and hidden under the scales of the head. They are burrowers and most of the 163 species also feed on ants and termites.

One species of blind snake, the Flowerpot snake, has spread from Asia to Europe by being carried in the earth in flowerpots. It is able to colonize a new area easily because the females can produce young on their own; there are no males.

6

5

3

4

A NARROW SQUEEZE

Like other reptiles, snakes have a head, body and tail, but the body, and sometimes the tail, are extremely long and narrow. The long body is supported by a very long backbone; some snakes have more than 400 vertebrae in the backbone. In such a body, it is difficult to fit in all the organs the snake needs. Often a pair of organs are one behind the other; the kidneys are positioned like this. Sometimes, only one of a pair of organs remains. Most snakes have just one lung.

◀The Costa Rican parrot snake is harmless, but can use its brightly colored mouth to frighten enemies.

SENSES

A snake is always staring and cannot shut its eyes because it has no eyelids. Instead the eyes are covered with a transparent scale. Burrowing snakes can usually just tell the difference between light and dark. In several daytime species, the eyesight is very sharp, although they find it much easier to see moving prey.

Night-time snakes frequently have vertical slit pupils which can open very wide in dim light to let in as much light as possible.

▼Snakes detect prey with their long forked tongues. This Toad-eater snake hunts on the forest floor in Costa Rica.

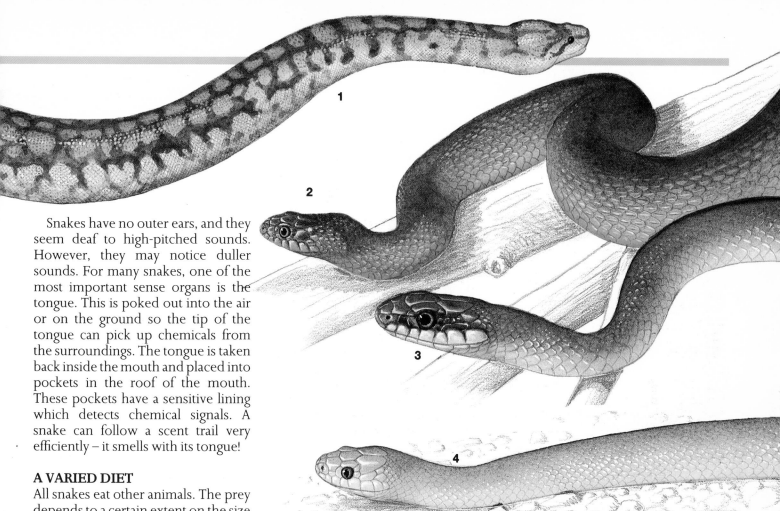

Snakes have no outer ears, and they seem deaf to high-pitched sounds. However, they may notice duller sounds. For many snakes, one of the most important sense organs is the tongue. This is poked out into the air or on the ground so the tip of the tongue can pick up chemicals from the surroundings. The tongue is taken back inside the mouth and placed into pockets in the roof of the mouth. These pockets have a sensitive lining which detects chemical signals. A snake can follow a scent trail very efficiently – it smells with its tongue!

A VARIED DIET

All snakes eat other animals. The prey depends to a certain extent on the size of the snake. Many eat mammals, birds or other reptiles, but some have a very special diet.

The tropical cat-eyed snakes and the Asian snail-eaters eat nothing but snails. They can pull a snail out of its shell. The African egg-eating snake eats eggs and can swallow an egg twice the size of its head. Part of its backbone sticks into its throat. To crack an egg, the snake squeezes it against this bone. The snake then swallows the contents of the egg and spits out the shell. The Redbelly snake of North America feeds exclusively on slugs. American green snakes eat caterpillars and grasshoppers. Perhaps a more typical diet, however, is that of the American garter snakes, which eat anything from worms and insects, to fish and mammals.

SWALLOWING DINNER

When snakes do feed, the meal is nearly always large compared with the size of the mouth. Food is always swallowed whole. A snake's teeth are sharp and point backwards.The teeth are good at holding food, but cannot bite off chunks of flesh. Instead, a snake has an amazingly flexible skull and jaws. It can open its mouth very wide. The bottom jaw can be swung down from the skull, and the two halves of the bottom jaw will swing apart, held together only by elastic tissue. The jaws can be "walked" around the prey, gradually edging it more and more into the throat, until contractions of the gullet can carry the food down to the stomach.

Those snakes of the family Colubridae that have fangs at the back of the mouth often "chew" on the prey. This probably helps them work in their poison, or venom. The most poisonous of these species includes the boomslang, an African tree snake. A

▲Harmless snakes Arafura wart snake (*Acrochordus arafurae*) (1) from rivers in New Guinea and Australia. Red-bellied water snake (*Nerodia erythrogaster*) (2) and the racer (*Coluber constrictor*) (3) from North America. The African house snake (*Lamprophis fuscus*) (4).

bite from this snake has proved fatal to a person in 24 hours.

A LONG SLOW LIFE

For much of the time, a snake's body works at a slow rate. Perhaps this is why they live for a long time. Even a small snake, such as a Milk snake, has been known to live for 18 years. Species of snake from cool areas may hibernate during the winter months. During this time they may be scarcely breathing and do not need to feed at all. Even during their active periods snakes are often still and can survive for long periods without a meal.

PYTHONS

In an African forest a hunter finds signs of a struggle. Worried, he peers into the surrounding trees. Suddenly there is a loud hiss and he draws back in alarm. When he looks again he sees a huge python. But this animal will do him no harm. It has just swallowed an antelope, and for the time being it can hardly move.

Some of the larger pythons have indeed been known to kill and eat people. Pythons are found in Africa, southern Asia and in the Australian region, which is especially rich in species. The exception is the Mexican burrowing python, which is only distantly related to other pythons.

LITTLE AND LARGE
Some of the pythons are giants among snakes, but there are small species

too. The dwarf python of Australia is less than 3ft long, and the Royal python of West Africa is only 5ft at most. The Royal python is also called the Ball python because it curls into a ball when it is alarmed. The Calabar python of West Africa is a burrowing species that grows to only about 3ft.

At the other extreme is the Reticulated python of South-east Asia, which is up to 33ft long. This is the longest snake in the world (but see Boas,

▼The Mexican burrowing python (1), the only python in the Americas, is rarely seen. When frightened, the Calabar python (2) curls up with its head on the inside and "strikes" with its tail.

PYTHONS Pythonidae
(*27 species*)

● ◻ 🐍

◼ Habitat: rain forest, thorn scrub and grassland.

◻ Diet: birds and mammals.

◎ Breeding: lay eggs in clutches of up to 60.

Size: most 10-20ft. Smallest (West Australian dwarf python): 20in long; largest (Reticulated python): 33ft.

Color: ranges from uniform brown or bright green to bold patterns of blotches or diamonds.

Species mentioned in text:
African rock python (*Python sebae*)
Calabar python (*Calabaria reinhardtii*)
Green tree python (*Chondropython viridis*)
Indian python (*Python molurus*)
Mexican burrowing python (*Loxocemus bicolor*)
Reticulated python (*Python reticulatus*)
Royal or Ball python (*P. regius*)
West Australian dwarf python (*Liasis perthensis*)
Woma (*Aspidites ramsayi*)

▲Some pythons coil round their eggs to guard them. Female Indian pythons may "shiver" to help keep their eggs warm.

◄The colors of the Green tree python match the leaves in the rain forest.

BABY COLORS

The Green tree python lives in the tropical forests of New Guinea and northern Australia. Its bright color is effective camouflage as it climbs and hunts in the trees. This helps it to move close to the animals it hunts without being seen. When the babies hatch from the egg, however, they are quite a different color. Some are yellowish; others are brick red. They have to wait for nearly 2 years before they become emerald green like the adults.

In other pythons, babies look much like the adults. A newly hatched Reticulated python is 24-30in long and weighs 5 ounces. It grows 24in a year for the first few years.

pages 66-67). Another giant is the Indian python, which has a thicker body than the Reticulated and grows up to 21½ft long. The African rock python can reach lengths of 30ft or more. These days few snakes are allowed to live long enough to reach their full size. With the current demand for snake skins for shoes, bags and wallets, the widespread use of rifles and the destruction of rain forests, large specimens are now rare.

SMALL AND LARGE MEALS

The Reticulated python feeds mainly on relatively small animals such as rats. In some places it is welcome because it destroys pests. The African rock python eats wild pigs and small antelopes. The Indian python tackles large animals, including leopards.

At the other extreme the West Australian dwarf python lives in termite nests and feeds on lizards which prey on the termites. The Australian woma eats many different animals, and can tackle poisonous snakes.

SPECIAL SENSES

As well as the usual snake senses, nearly all pythons have a series of special "pits" along the jaws. These pits are sensitive to heat. Pythons may use these pits to help them detect small animals, such as rats or birds, which are warmer than their surroundings. The snakes can determine temperature differences of $\frac{1}{1,000}°F$ and so locate prey in total darkness.

▼This African rock python has killed a gazelle and is beginning to swallow it. It may be weeks before it feeds again.

BOAS

In a Brazilian river, all is quiet. A caiman lazes at the surface. Suddenly there is a flurry in the water. From a branch above, an anaconda seizes the caiman. There is a struggle as the caiman tries to break free and the anaconda tries to wind its coils around the caiman's body. Eventually the anaconda succeeds, and squeezes the caiman until it is dead.

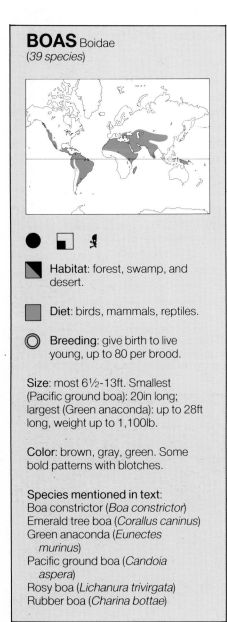

BOAS Boidae
(39 species)

● ■ 🦂

◨ Habitat: forest, swamp, and desert.

■ Diet: birds, mammals, reptiles.

◎ Breeding: give birth to live young, up to 80 per brood.

Size: most 6½-13ft. Smallest (Pacific ground boa): 20in long; largest (Green anaconda): up to 28ft long, weight up to 1,100lb.

Color: brown, gray, green. Some bold patterns with blotches.

Species mentioned in text:
Boa constrictor (*Boa constrictor*)
Emerald tree boa (*Corallus caninus*)
Green anaconda (*Eunectes murinus*)
Pacific ground boa (*Candoia aspera*)
Rosy boa (*Lichanura trivirgata*)
Rubber boa (*Charina bottae*)

Like the pythons (see pages 64-65), boas catch their prey by constriction. They strike and seize animals with their sharp backward-pointing teeth, then wrap their bodies around the victim. Powerful muscles squeeze the prey and stop it from breathing. When the prey is dead, it is swallowed whole, usually head first so that it slides down more easily.

A VARIED DIET

Boas have a scattered distribution. Their main home is in Central and South America, where there are some 20 species, but the small Rosy and Rubber boas live in western North America. Boas also occur on New Guinea, and some Pacific islands. Sand boas live in western Asia and north Africa, and there are three species on Madagascar.

Most boas feed on rat-sized prey. Some specialize in catching roosting birds and bats. Many boas have well-developed heat-sensing pits on their lips. With these they can detect small differences in temperature between an object and its surroundings and so can locate prey by their body heat. The anaconda eats mainly mammals, but also feeds on caimans and turtles.

HEAVIEST SNAKE

Most boas are not enormous. They tend to have slender bodies and longer tails than pythons. The Common boa, or Boa constrictor, of South and Central America, is one of the larger species. It is rarely more than 10ft long, but a few reach over 16½ft. It lives in forests, and climbs well, but can also be found in some dry areas.

The giant of the family is the Green or Common anaconda, which lives in and around water. One large individual was well over 26½ft long. There are sometimes reports of anacondas which measure 36ft or more, but these stories are rarely well documented and so far none of them has been proven true by scientists. An anaconda this size would be longer than the longest python. However, an anaconda is a heavy, wide-bodied snake, and even one 26½ft long is much heavier than any python.

CLIMBERS AND BURROWERS

Many of the boas are small lightweight tree-climbers. Most remarkable in its feeding habits is the Emerald tree boa, which looks very much like the Green tree python. It feeds largely on birds, and has long front teeth which help it to seize birds from tree branches.

A totally different life is led by the sand boas, which burrow in sand and soil in dry areas of Africa and Asia. They have rounded bodies, a nose like a shovel and blunt tails. They reach a maximum length of 3ft, but are often only half this length. They stay in burrows during the day, and capture mice on the surface at night. The Rubber boa burrows in damp forests in the western USA. It is up to 24in long and feeds on mice and lizards.

GIVING BIRTH

Boas are similar to pythons in many ways, but one big difference is that boas do not lay eggs. Instead, they all give birth to live young. After the babies are born, the mother does not look after them. Baby Boa constrictors are 12in long at birth. Newborn anacondas may be twice this length.

SNAKES WITH LEGS

Boas and pythons differ from most other snakes in that they still have two lungs, although one is much larger than the other. They also have traces of hind legs. Inside the body are tiny leg bones, and on the outside are two claws. These seem almost useless, but they are larger in males and are used to stroke females during courtship.

▶ The Emerald tree boa from South America grips a tree tightly with its prehensile tail as it prepares to swallow a bird whole. The snake had struck, then squeezed the bird until it died.

COBRAS

The snake charmer takes the lid off a basket and sits back. He begins to play a pipe. From the basket the head of a cobra rises, with its hood spread out. As the charmer plays, he sways backwards and forwards, and the snake "dances." It is worried, dazzled by the sudden brightness, and is trying to keep in view the strange moving object, the pipe end.

When disturbed, cobras rise up and spread special thin neck ribs to tighten loose skin into a "hood." Cobras and their relations are poisonous snakes found throughout Africa and southern Asia. Their American relatives are the coral snakes (see pages 72-73). In these regions the cobra family is only a small part of the total number of snake species. But in Australia, cobras and their relatives make up 80 per cent of the snakes. There, poisonous snakes outnumber the harmless ones.

VENOM

In members of the cobra family, some of the salivary glands have become modified to produce venom, which is used to paralyze and kill prey. The venom contains a mixture of poisons, but substances that act on the nervous system are the most common. These poisons give rise to breathing or heart problems or paralysis. Most of these snakes have a bite which is dangerous to people; the venom is often effective within only an hour of being injected.

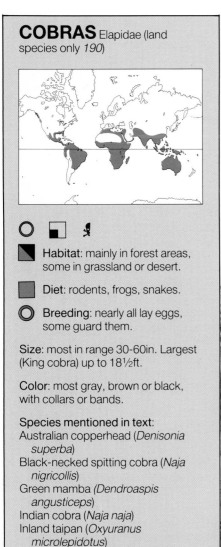

COBRAS Elapidae (land species only *190*)

○ ◻ ☠

◼ Habitat: mainly in forest areas, some in grassland or desert.

◼ Diet: rodents, frogs, snakes.

◎ Breeding: nearly all lay eggs, some guard them.

Size: most in range 30-60in. Largest (King cobra) up to 18½ft.

Color: most gray, brown or black, with collars or bands.

Species mentioned in text:
Australian copperhead (*Denisonia superba*)
Black-necked spitting cobra (*Naja nigricollis*)
Green mamba (*Dendroaspis angusticeps*)
Indian cobra (*Naja naja*)
Inland taipan (*Oxyuranus microlepidotus*)
King cobra (*Ophiophagus hannah*)
Ringhals (*Hemachatus haemachatus*)
Taipan (*Oxyuranus scutellatus*)
Tiger snake (*Notechis scutatus*)

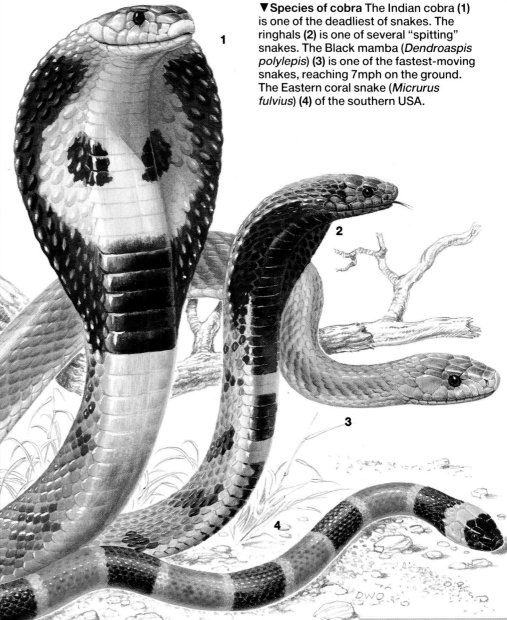

▼Species of cobra The Indian cobra (1) is one of the deadliest of snakes. The ringhals (2) is one of several "spitting" snakes. The Black mamba (*Dendroaspis polylepis*) (3) is one of the fastest-moving snakes, reaching 7mph on the ground. The Eastern coral snake (*Micrurus fulvius*) (4) of the southern USA.

Cobras have short fangs which are a pair of special, needle-like, upper teeth. When the snakes strike, they usually hold on to make sure the venom is injected into their victim. The fangs are hollow, with a channel down the middle to carry the venom. Like most other snakes, cobras are not usually aggressive, and try to avoid trouble from their enemies – mostly people, birds of prey and mongooses. Their venom is usually saved for its proper job – helping to catch animals to eat. But cobras are common in parts of the world where people often go

▲ A baby Green mamba uses its snout to break the parchment-like eggshell.

▼ A female cobra incubates her eggs by coiling around them.

barefoot, and each year they kill many people. Cobras, though, can often deter enemies without biting them by spraying venom, raising their hood or using their skin coloration as a warning signal.

SPRAY OF POISON

Three species of cobra can "spit" their venom in defense. The channel in each fang which carries the venom opens at the front of the tooth instead of at the tip. Muscles squeeze a stream of venom droplets up to 10ft away from the open mouth. The cobra usually aims the venom at the eyes, causing irritation or blindness to the attacker. This gives the snake time to escape. The most effective sprayer of venom is probably the ringhals, a small cobra only about 3ft long. If this snake is alarmed, it will sometimes "play dead" and loll with its mouth open. If this does not work, it will spray venom at an enemy.

COBRA HOODS

Most true cobras live in Africa, but one species, the Indian cobra, lives in southern Asia. The hood of true cobras is made from skin supported by long ribs. For much of the time a cobra looks as thin-necked as any other snake. However, when it is alarmed, it spreads the neck ribs so that the hood is extended. In some cobras there are marks that resemble "eyes" on the hood to make it appear more frightening. A displaying cobra may frighten off attacking animals without having to strike them with venom. Mambas, which are African members of the cobra family, have no hood, but can inflate the throat when they are irritated.

KING OF THE SNAKES

The King cobra or hamadryad is not only the largest cobra, but also the largest venomous snake. When it rears up, its head can be level with a person's head. It lives over much of

India and South-east Asia, but is not very common. The hamadryad has a powerful venom and a reputation for sometimes being aggressive. It feeds mostly on other snakes.

STRIPY SNAKES

Coral snakes have bands of bright red, yellow, white and black along the body. True coral snakes are found in the Americas, but other similarly colored snakes are found in Africa, Asia and Australia. They are all rather secretive, living under logs or leaf litter, or even underground.

The function of the bright colors of coral snakes seems to be to startle any enemy that finds them. Although these species are mostly small, they have a powerful venom. The fangs are small, so often they have to inflict several bites to be effective. Many kinds eat other snakes.

CONTINENT OF KILLERS

Australian snakes include some of the most venomous land snakes. The taipan, which grows up to 11ft, is the largest. It has a reputation for being particularly aggressive. Luckily it is not very common. The Inland taipan has perhaps the most potent venom of any land snake. One specimen was found to contain enough venom to kill 125,000 mice. The Tiger snake is much more common and has an extremely dangerous venom.

EGGS AND BABIES

Most cobras lay eggs, but the ringhals of Africa and several Australian species produce live young. The Tiger snake may produce as many as 50 babies in a litter. The Australian copperhead even has a type of placenta through which the babies are nourished inside their mother. Typically, all the young are born or hatch between 3 and 4 months after mating takes place.

Some species of cobra have more of a family life than is usual among snakes. A few curl around the eggs and guard them. Male and female Indian cobras may help to dig out a nest hole and defend the eggs. The King cobra has the most elaborate care of all. The female scrapes together a large pile of leaves, grass and soil to make a nest. She makes a hole in the top of the pile, lays 20 to 40 eggs in the hollow and covers them with more leaves. Then she stays on guard on the nest until the eggs hatch. The male may also stay close by and help to drive off enemies.

Baby cobras are small versions of their parents, and are able to spread the hood, rear their heads and deliver a venomous bite from the moment of hatching.

▼A Black-necked spitting cobra of South Africa ejects its poisonous spray. The poison is usually aimed at its victim's eyes and can cause permanent blindness.

▶A mamba wrapping itself round the branches of a thorn bush. Many cobras are excellent tree-climbers and some can even scale the thin upright trunks of bamboo.

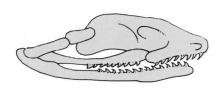

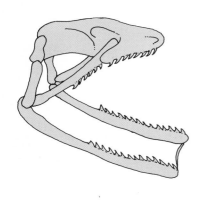

▲Snakes can open their mouth wide because the lower jaw is connected to the skull by hinge-like bones. Also, ligaments stretched between bones are extremely elastic.

SEA-SNAKES

A snake swims through the clear blue water near a coral reef. It moves slowly and easily, looking around. As it pauses to peer into a crevice, it spots an eel lurking inside. The snake shoots out its head and with its teeth fastens on to the fish. The fish stiffens, then flops lifeless. The sea-snake has caught another meal.

SEA-SNAKES Elapidae
(marine species only *about 50*)

Habitat: mainly shallow tropical seas.

Diet: fishes; some species eat only eels or fish eggs.

Breeding: most give birth in water to live young; a few lay eggs on land.

Size: most about 4½ft long; largest up to 8¼ft.

Color: varied. Some rather dull; others banded light and dark, some black and yellow or black and red.

Species mentioned in text:
Banded sea-snake (*Laticauda colubrina*)
Black-and-yellow sea-snake (*Pelamis platurus*)
Red-and-black sea-snake (*Astrotia stokesi*)

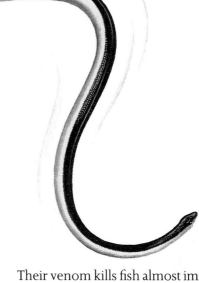

► The Black-and-yellow sea-snake is flattened from side to side. It has been seen hundreds of miles from land.

◄ Totally at home in the water, a Banded sea-snake hunts across the sea bed near the New Hebrides in the Pacific.

Most sea-snakes live all their lives in salt water. Sea-snakes are commonest in the south-west Pacific from Malaysia to Australia, but a few kinds live in the seas north to Japan, east to the Solomon Islands and west to Saudi Arabia. Most sea-snakes are found in shallow seas relatively close to the coast. The exception is the Black-and-yellow sea-snake, which is found right out in the ocean, from East Africa to the eastern Pacific.

ALL AT SEA

Sea-snakes are closely related to the cobras, and have short fixed front fangs too. But, in several ways, they are specially adapted for the sea. Most do not have the large belly scales usually found in land snakes, as they do not need them to help grip the ground. They have valves on their nostrils which they can shut to keep out the water. The lungs are large, sometimes running almost the complete length of the body, and can act as floats as well as for breathing. Tails are flattened from side to side to help push the snake through the water.

Some sea-snakes have a very small head, a long thin neck and a fat body. These species put their head into rock crevices to catch small eels.

POWERFUL POISONS

Some species of sea-snakes have the most powerful venom of any snake. They need to overcome prey quickly before it escapes into the vast ocean.

Their venom kills fish almost immediately. Several sea-snakes eat fish eggs. Others eat soft-bodied sea animals. But their usual food seems to be fish, mainly eels, perhaps because these are an easy shape to swallow. Luckily, sea-snakes are placid and rarely bite people, even when they throw the snakes out of their fishing nets by hand. However, a bite may well be fatal to humans.

MYSTERIOUS LIVES

Most sea-snakes are unable to move on land, and so cannot come ashore to lay eggs. Instead, they give birth to live young. One small group, which includes the Banded sea-snake, can crawl on land, and does lay eggs, often in caves above the tide level. Sea-snakes may occasionally and briefly rest on islets, but otherwise they live in water all the time.

Sea-snakes sometimes gather in vast numbers. It is thought this may be for breeding, but little is known about much of sea-snakes' lives. In 1932, a huge gathering was recorded by a ship which steamed for 65 miles past a "solid mass" of sea-snakes about 10ft wide. They were all of the Red-and-black species, and there must have been many millions of individuals.

VIPERS AND RATTLESNAKES

It is a pitch-dark night out on the prairie. A mouse scurries about, intent on finding seeds. In a hollow lies a rattlesnake. It cannot see the mouse, but it senses the presence of its warm body. It turns its head towards the mouse, waits until it is close, then strikes. It stabs and injects venom, then settles back to wait for its victim's death.

Vipers and rattlesnakes have the best-developed fangs of all the snakes. Members of this family live in all parts of the world that are warm enough for snakes, except for Madagascar and the Australian region. There are two main groups. The 45 species of true viper live in Africa, Europe and Asia. The 142 species of pit viper (including rattlesnakes) live in the Americas and southern Asia.

Instead of the big head shields seen in most other snakes, snakes of this family usually have triangular heads covered with many small scales. The body is thick, and often quite short. The eyes have slit-like pupils.

BIG FANGS
Vipers have a pair of very long fangs. In a Gaboon viper 5½ft long, the fangs can be 2in long. When a viper is at rest, the fangs are folded back against the roof of the mouth. When it strikes, the mouth is opened wide and the fangs are swung down into a stabbing position.

Many vipers and rattlesnakes stab their prey, give a quick injection of powerful venom, then let go. There is no need to hang on. The prey soon dies, and even if it has moved a little way off, the snake can track it down and find it. Because of their shape and

VIPERS AND RATTLESNAKES
Viperidae (*187 species*)

○ ◨ ⚚

◼ **Habitat:** all types, from tropical rain forest, to grassland, desert, mountain and moors.

◼ **Diet:** other animals.

◎ **Breeding:** most give birth to small number of live young. Some have up to 50 per litter. Some lay eggs.

Size: most 24-48in. Smallest (Peringuey's viper): 12in long; longest (bushmaster): up to 12¼ft long.

Color: generally dull colors, brown or blackish, often with dark blotches on lighter background. Some with bright colors or markings.

Species mentioned in text:
Bushmaster (*Lachesis muta*)
European adder (*Vipera berus*)
Gaboon viper (*Bitis gabonica*)
Hog-nosed viper (*Bothrops nasutus*)
Peringuey's viper (*Bitis peringueyi*)
Side-winder rattlesnake (*Crotalus cerastes*)
Western diamondback rattlesnake (*C. atrox*)
Western rattlesnake (*C. viridis*)

▶ On the Wyoming prairie, a Western rattlesnake hides in low brush, ready to strike a passing lizard or hare.

the way their fangs work, vipers are best suited to ambushing their prey rather than chasing it.

DEADLY POISONS

The venom of vipers is not so strong as that of some snakes in the cobra family (see pages 68-71), but it is made in such quantities, and is so efficiently injected, that it does its work well.

Many vipers are capable of killing a person, but they are less aggressive than cobras and are often slow to anger. Some small species, such as the European adder, have a bite that is painful to people, but is rarely fatal. Viper venoms act mainly on the blood and muscle systems, causing pain, swelling, severe bruising, discoloration and other acute symptoms. Recovery may be slow.

HEAT DETECTORS

The major difference between pit vipers and true vipers can be seen in the face. Pit vipers have a pair of large pits below the eyes. Each pit has a membrane inside which can detect heat; it can detect a heat difference of just $2/5°F$.

Warm-blooded prey can be sensed with these pits. The snake can line up its head on prey, even in complete darkness, by turning the head so that the same amount of warmth is detected by each pit. A rattlesnake can detect and strike a mouse nearly 3ft away with deadly accuracy, even in total darkness.

RATTLE AND BUZZ

Rattlesnakes are found in the Americas. The rattle on the tip of the tail is

▲ After injecting venom for the kill, the two fangs of the Hog-nosed viper help to pull a frog into the snake's mouth.

▲ Below the eye and nostril of this rattlesnake can be seen the large pit which acts as a heat detector.

made of a series of hollow, horny tail-tips. Like other snakes, a rattle-snake sheds its skin at intervals, but the horny tip of the tail remains permanently in place.

Each time the snake sheds its skin, a new segment is added to the rattle. Many snakes shake the tail if they are alarmed or annoyed; this may make a sound by hitting against and rustling leaves or dry plants. But, if rattlesnakes are disturbed, the tail itself makes a loud, angry buzzing noise. The snake cannot hear the noise, but it can scare off enemies and is a useful method of defense. A rattlesnake's main enemies are foxes and birds of prey.

◄Peringuey's viper of southern Africa leaves characteristic parallel tracks as it moves swiftly across the sand by "sidewinding."

SPRINGING SIDEWAYS

Several vipers and rattlesnakes are adapted to living in deserts. These snakes are often a sandy color, and may bury themselves in the sand so that only their eyes show above the surface. Many of these desert-living snakes have "horns" over their eyes, which may help to keep the sand out of their pupils.

Some of these desert vipers, and the Side-winder rattlesnake, have a special way of traveling over the sand. It is hard for the snakes to grip the sand to pull themselves along, and, in the middle of the day, the sand may be burningly hot. So the snakes move by

▼Rattlesnakes, such as this Western diamondback, strike prey or an attacker with the mouth wide open and the long fangs erect.

"side-winding," which allows them to touch the sand as little as possible.

A side-winding snake makes an arc with the front part of its body and "throws" its head sideways for some distance before it touches the sand. The rest of the body is then thrown forward in another arc, clear of the ground, so it lands in front of the head. The tail curves over and lands last, but by this time the head has already been thrown to a new position and the body follows. The effect is rather like a spring rolling sideways.

Side-winding is weird to watch, but is an effective, and quite speedy, way of traveling across sand. It is mostly used by vipers of African and North American deserts. A very character-istic series of marks, each shaped rather like a "J," is left behind by the snake as it "side-winds" over the sand.

WORM-LIZARDS

A Mexican worker is digging a trench through the earth. As he exposes some new soil, a pink worm appears. When he bends down to look at it, the "worm" suddenly produces two legs close behind the head, and wriggles away into the soft earth. It is a burrowing reptile, a Mexican worm-lizard, which the worker has disturbed in its underground home.

Worm-lizards are found mainly in Africa. Some live in the warmer parts of the Americas, others are found in Arabia, western Asia, and southern Europe. They are one of the strangest kinds of reptile and, because of the way they live, little is known about their lives.

For a long time, nobody knew quite what to make of these animals. In the past, they were classified both as snakes and lizards. Like snakes, they have only one lung, but it is the left lung, instead of the right lung, as in snakes. Nowadays, worm-lizards are classified in a separate group of their own. From fossils, we know they have been living on the Earth for at least 65 million years.

UNDERGROUND TUNNELS

Worm-lizards spend almost all their time underground. They make their own tunnels, many of them in very hard soils. Their bodies have many things which help them to burrow efficiently. Most worm-lizards have lost all trace of front and back legs. The exceptions are the Mexican worm-lizards, which have two short, strong front legs with five-clawed toes.

Worm-lizards all closely resemble worms, with their long bodies (usually without legs), their generally small size, and also in the look of the skin. They do have scales, but these are small and arranged in rings around the body, giving a segmented appearance like an earthworm. The skin is quite loosely attached to the body, and can slide over it easily. To crawl forwards through its tunnels, the animal fixes part of the skin against the tunnel wall and pulls up the rest of its body in a series of waves.

A worm-lizard is able to reverse the direction of the muscles attached to the rings, so that it can go backwards through the soil too. On some species it is difficult to see which is the head and which is the tail. Their scientific name means "those who move in both directions."

THICK HEADS

A worm-lizard makes its tunnels by pushing its head through the soil. The skull is extremely hard, strong and solid and it is used like a battering ram. The snout may be blunt and round or shaped like a shovel, as in the Florida worm-lizard. The scales on the snout may be strengthened, or they may be slippery so the worm-lizard can push its way through the soil.

To tap the soil into place in the tunnel walls, a worm-lizard moves its head and neck upwards and sideways. This leaves a channel along which the animal can pull itself in its accordion-like fashion. Worm-lizards do not need to push soil to the surface.

▲The Mexican worm-lizard has tiny forelimbs which can be used to scrape soil when starting a burrow.

EYES AND EARS

As worm-lizards mainly live underground, they have little use for eyes. The eyes are small and below the surface of the skin. There are no ear openings on the outside, but the ear bones are connected to the jaws and worm-lizards seem to be able to hear sounds coming down their tunnels.

A FIERCE BITE

Worm-lizards are ferocious predators. Sharp, large teeth are fixed in their short jaws, which clamp together hard

▲Worm-lizards have small eyes beneath the skin, no outside ear openings, and nostrils that point backward so that pressure closes them during burrowing.

and may crush prey or tear it apart as it is pulled back down the tunnel. Insects are the main food, but worms and some larger animals are eaten. Worm-lizards recognize their prey by sound and perhaps by scent. They may drink by sucking water from the soil between their lips and tongue,

but also get liquid from their prey.

Worm-lizards are often found in ant or termite nests, and these insects may be their main food. Some species also lay their eggs in ants' nests. As the embryos grow, they become very long and fold themselves up in a tight spiral within the eggs.

TUATARA

As the Sun moves higher in the sky, scuffling noises can be heard from a seabird's breeding burrow on an islet off New Zealand. But it's not a bird that emerges into the sunlight. It is a reptile, a tuatara, coming out to bask in the Sun. Traces of egg around its jaws show that it has raided a nest down the burrow, besides using it as a shelter.

Tuataras are relics of a bygone age. They are found only in isolated parts of New Zealand. Some of their most unusual features are a "third eye" on top of the head, eggs that take 15 months to hatch and a lifespan of over 100 years.

"Tuatara" is a Maori word meaning "peaks on the back." This refers to the crest of triangular folds of skin along the back and tail of the animal. The crest is well-developed in the male, but small in the female. It is usually soft and floppy, but males can raise and stiffen their crests when they are alarmed. This acts as a threat display. Female tuataras are very timid and retreat hastily when disturbed.

LIVING FOSSIL
The tuatara is the only surviving member of a group of reptiles that came into being 220 million years ago, before the first dinosaurs. These reptiles lived almost all over the world, but nearly all died out before the end of the Age of Dinosaurs. Animals almost identical to the tuatara were living 140 million years ago. Perhaps the tuatara can give us clues about the life of reptiles in those far-off days.

AN EXTRA EYE
The tuatara has part of the brain connected to a well-developed "third eye" on top of the head. This eye has a lens and is sensitive to light, but it cannot form images like a true eye. It may be very important as a kind of light meter to help the tuatara control its basking behavior.

A SLOW LIFE
The tuatara's body seems to work rather slowly, even for a reptile. But unlike many reptiles, it can be active at low body temperatures, even down to 50°F. It lays eggs, and these can take longer to hatch than those of any other back-boned animal. Growth is slow, yet may continue for a long time. Tuataras become sexually mature at about 20 years old, but may still be growing at 60 years old. If tuataras survive to become adults, they can almost certainly expect to live for 120 years. Some people believe that tuataras may reach ages of 200 or more, but this has never been proved.

They mate in summer. The following spring the female digs a burrow and lays her eggs. The next year they hatch. The hatchlings are about 4in long and very active. They may dig small burrows for themselves, or hide

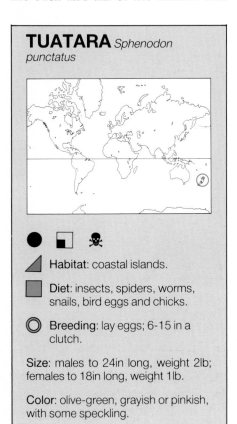

TUATARA *Sphenodon punctatus*

● ◰ ☠

◣ Habitat: coastal islands.

▪ Diet: insects, spiders, worms, snails, bird eggs and chicks.

○ Breeding: lay eggs; 6-15 in a clutch.

Size: males to 24in long, weight 2lb; females to 18in long, weight 1lb.

Color: olive-green, grayish or pinkish, with some speckling.

▼The crest that runs from neck to tail gives the tuatara its name, which means "peaks on the back" in Maori.

under logs and stones. They have to feed and protect themselves.

REPTILE OF DARKNESS

Tuataras come out of their burrows on sunny days to warm up in the Sun. They are also active at night.

Tuataras spend much of their time in burrows. They can dig these burrows themselves, but often live in the nesting burrows of petrels or other seabirds. As well as providing the tuatara with a ready-made shelter, these birds produce dung that attracts the beetles and other insects which the tuatara eats. Sometimes tuataras may eat seabird eggs or chicks. They also feed on other small animals, such as spiders, worms and snails, and on small lizards.

ON THE ROCKS

The tuatara used to live on the two main islands of New Zealand. Now it is found only on about 30 rock stacks and small islands off the New Zealand coast. The islands are difficult to land on, and this helps to protect the tuatara from people. Its worst enemy is the rat, which will eat tuatara eggs and young. The most successful colonies are on rat-free islands. Throughout its range, the tuatara is now fully protected by law, which is essential for its survival.

▼ The tuatara is endangered. Less than half the islands where it lives now have thriving breeding populations.

ALLIGATORS

A big female alligator slips into the water. She has a mouth full of small animals. When she is in the water, she opens her mouth wide and the small animals swim off to hide in the reeds. They are baby alligators. Their mother goes back to the nest for another batch of hatchlings. She continues until all her babies are safely in the water.

Alligators, and their close relatives the crocodiles (see pages 86-89), are unusual for reptiles in that the parents care for their young. Alligators are found in south-eastern North America. Their close family relatives, the caimans, are found in Central and South America. On the other side of the world, in China, lives the Chinese alligator. This species is found, in small numbers, in the Chang Jiang River. It is so far away from other members of the alligator family that western scientists did not believe the first reports of its existence.

▼ Most alligators come out of the water to bask from time to time. These American alligators are warming up on a mud bank in Georgia, USA.

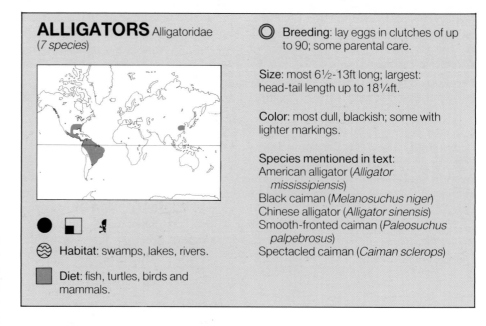

ALLIGATORS Alligatoridae
(*7 species*)

○ Breeding: lay eggs in clutches of up to 90; some parental care.

Size: most 6½-13ft long; largest: head-tail length up to 18¼ft.

Color: most dull, blackish; some with lighter markings.

Species mentioned in text:
American alligator (*Alligator mississipiensis*)
Black caiman (*Melanosuchus niger*)
Chinese alligator (*Alligator sinensis*)
Smooth-fronted caiman (*Paleosuchus palpebrosus*)
Spectacled caiman (*Caiman sclerops*)

● ◻ ⚡

≋ Habitat: swamps, lakes, rivers.

◻ Diet: fish, turtles, birds and mammals.

CROCODILE OR ALLIGATOR?

Crocodiles and alligators – together known as crocodilians – are similar, and have many features in common, but a few things set them apart. The animals in the alligator family often have a broad snout; crocodiles usually bear a long snout. Many alligators have bony plates in the skin of the belly; crocodiles do not. When alligators close their mouths, the fourth tooth in each side of the lower jaw fits into a socket in the upper jaw so it cannot be seen. In crocodiles, this pair of teeth sticks up outside the top jaw when the mouth is closed.

A WATERY LIFE

Alligators live in and around water. Their eyes and nostrils are set high on the head so that they can see and breathe when they are almost totally submerged. A third eyelid can be drawn across the eye to give more protection during diving. This eyelid is transparent and does not interfere

with the animal's sharp vision. When alligators and crocodiles dive underwater, they can close their nostrils and their ears. Out of the water their hearing seems good.

One important adaptation to diving is the flap of skin which shuts off the mouth from the breathing tubes. This allows the animal to open its mouth underwater to catch and eat prey, without water getting into its lungs.

GETTING ABOUT

All crocodilians have a large, strong tail with flat sides, which is used to push the animal through the water. The legs may steer or balance a little, but they are often folded back when the animal swims. The back legs are longer than the front legs.

Some crocodilians move only a short distance from water. Others may travel some distance overland when

▼The Chinese alligator was not known to western scientists until 1879. It is a rare animal. It grows to a maximum length of 6ft and has a short snout.

▲The Spectacled caiman of South America gets its name from the ridge between the eye sockets. This one is swallowing a fish that it has caught.

▼The American alligator occurs in wet habitats in the southern States. During cold winter periods it may dig a mud hole in which to hibernate.

they need to. Sometimes they crawl or slither, but many species can also do a "high walk" with the body raised off the ground and their weight supported by the legs. Some can move fast, or even gallop. The American alligator is generally slow-moving. Compared with many crocodilians, and even its relatives the caimans, it is rather clumsy. It is rarely aggressive.

AMERICAN ALLIGATORS

American alligators eat mostly slow-moving fish, but their prey also includes any birds, mammals, reptiles and amphibians that they can surprise in the water. Large alligators can kill people, though they are not usually interested in attacking humans. American alligators have been known to eat pets when houses have been built near the swamps where they live.

Male alligators are larger than the females, but most individuals do not grow more than 10ft long. The record length is for a specimen from Louisiana that was measured at 19¼ft. Few present-day individuals approach the size of such giants.

CAIMANS

The largest of the caimans is the Black caiman, which can grow to 11½ft or more. In the 19th century, individuals of over 16½ft long could be found. It is black above, yellowish beneath. The Black caiman lives in the Amazon and Orinoco regions of South America. At the other extreme is the Smooth-fronted caiman, which grows to a maximum length of only 5ft. It is found mostly in rocky, fast-running streams.

Caimans have sharper, longer teeth than alligators and strong bony plates on the belly and back. These belly plates have made the animals less attractive to people to hunt for making leather goods than some of the other crocodilians. Like all their relatives, caimans have about 40 pointed teeth in use at any one time.

NESTS AND BABIES

The bellow of a male alligator sounds like thunder and may help him to attract a mate. Mating takes place in the water. When the female is ready to lay her eggs, she makes a nest out of mud and vegetation. The nest may be 3ft high and 6½ft across. After she has laid her eggs, the mother remains on top of the nest to guard the eggs from enemies. The rotting vegetation produces some heat, which helps to keep the eggs warm. After about 9 weeks, the babies are ready to hatch and call out. The mother alligator hears their calls and tears open the nest. She picks up the babies in her mouth and takes them to the water. Sometimes this will be a "nursery pool" which she has dug herself. As the young grow, the mother continues to guard them, for up to a year.

GROWING UP

Many animals will eat alligator eggs or babies if given the chance. Luckily the baby alligators grow fast. At hatching they may be only 8in long, but will grow some 12in a year for the first few years. After about 9 years, their rate of growth slows down. An alligator may be 8 years old before it can breed. The maximum possible lifespan may be 100 years.

SAFE FROM EXTINCTION

At one time, the American alligator was seriously endangered. This was partly because it was hunted for its skin and flesh and partly through the loss of its habitat as swamps were drained for farming or for building. This species has, however, been so well protected for the last few years that numbers have now increased to several million. There are so many individuals that controlled hunting is now allowed in some states.

► In the water, a large American alligator can move with very little effort, gliding through its swampy home.

CROCODILES

At the water's edge a group of antelope are drinking. A few yards out in the water, a pair of eyes and a nose are the only signs that a crocodile is hunting. Gently it glides towards the bank. With a sudden lunge, it grabs an antelope by the leg, and pulls it into the water. The crocodile holds the antelope underwater until it drowns, then tears off chunks of flesh to eat.

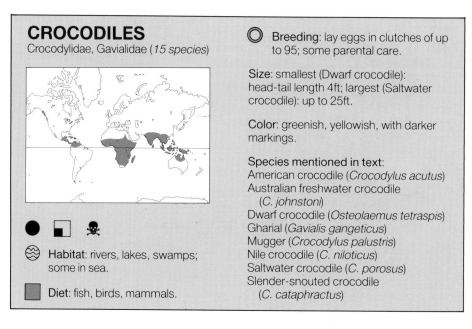

CROCODILES
Crocodylidae, Gavialidae (*15 species*)

○ Breeding: lay eggs in clutches of up to 95; some parental care.

Size: smallest (Dwarf crocodile): head-tail length 4ft; largest (Saltwater crocodile): up to 25ft.

Color: greenish, yellowish, with darker markings.

Species mentioned in text:
American crocodile (*Crocodylus acutus*)
Australian freshwater crocodile
  (*C. johnstoni*)
Dwarf crocodile (*Osteolaemus tetraspis*)
Gharial (*Gavialis gangeticus*)
Mugger (*Crocodylus palustris*)
Nile crocodile (*C. niloticus*)
Saltwater crocodile (*C. porosus*)
Slender-snouted crocodile
  (*C. cataphractus*)

⊗ Habitat: rivers, lakes, swamps; some in sea.

◼ Diet: fish, birds, mammals.

Crocodiles are fearsome predators. Some 14 species live in Africa, tropical parts of Asia and Australia, and in America from southern Florida to northern South America.

One species, the gharial, is found only in the great river systems of northern India. It is also the odd one out among these reptiles on account of its extremely long, narrow snout and weak legs. It is grouped in a separate family of its own, Gavialidae.

MEATY MENUS
Crocodiles with long snouts, such as the Slender-snouted crocodile, feed mainly on fish.

Species with broader snouts, such as the mugger, tackle bigger prey, including deer and cattle. The Nile crocodile may feed on all sorts of animals from fishes to zebras. In fact, the diet of a crocodile often varies through its lifetime. Newly hatched crocodiles feed on small items such as grasshoppers, but as they grow they start to eat frogs and small fish. Eventually they move on to larger fish, and mammals such as antelopes.

1

The long, thin jaws of the gharial, which are full of pointed teeth, are ideal for snapping at fish in the water. The gharial specializes in eating fish.

HIDDEN KILLERS

Crocodiles usually take their prey by surprise. Most crocodiles are well camouflaged, and will stay completely still, or move slowly towards their prey without being detected.

Crocodile teeth are good for seizing and holding, but not so good at cutting up or chewing prey. To pull apart large prey, which cannot be swallowed whole, crocodiles make twisting movements of the whole body to tear off chunks of meat. Crocodiles may often lose teeth while dealing with prey, but this does not matter, as they are constantly growing new ones. A Nile crocodile 13ft long is probably using its 45th "set" of teeth.

Crocodiles swim using their powerful tails, which have flattened sides. On land they often slither along on their bellies, but can also walk with the body lifted clear of the ground.

▼Species of crocodile Dwarf crocodile (1) of forest areas of West Africa and the Congo. The False gharial (*Tomistoma schlegeli*) (2), a fish-eater of swamps and rivers in Malaya, Borneo and Sumatra. The gharial (3) from northern India. The Slender-snouted crocodile (4) of African tropical forests. The mugger (5) of India lives in rivers, pools and marshes. American crocodile (6).

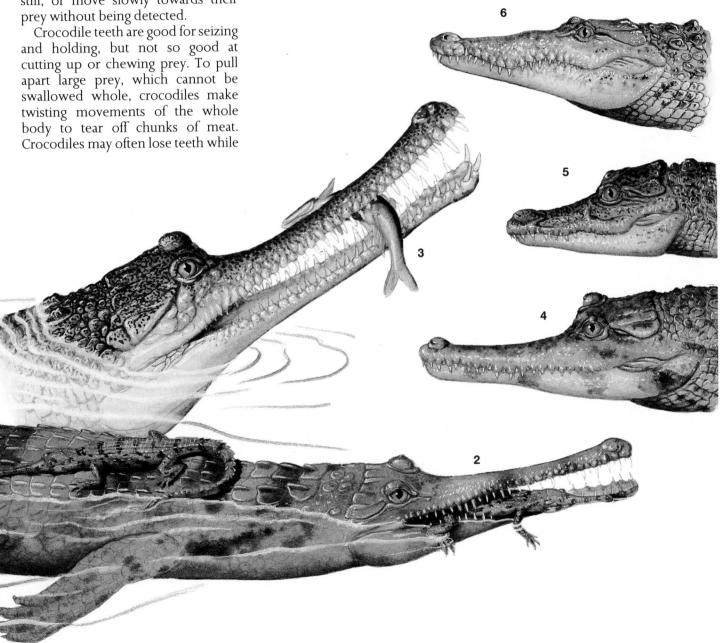

Some crocodiles can even gallop, reaching speeds of 8mph. They are all most active at night. Much of the day may be spent basking. When crocodiles are hot they open their jaws and lose water from the skin inside the mouth to cool themselves. The Nile crocodile, when it is basking open-mouthed, will allow birds to pick over its teeth for scraps of food.

SEA-GOING CROCODILES

Crocodiles of several species may venture into estuaries or the sea. The American crocodile often lives in brackish swamps, and may swim out to sea. The Nile crocodile is found in estuaries in parts of Africa. But the most sea-loving of all crocodiles is the Saltwater crocodile, which is found in estuaries and mangrove swamps. Around Indonesia, some individuals may live in the sea all the time. The Saltwater crocodile is a strong swimmer. Stray animals have reached the Cocos-Keeling Islands, 560 miles from their usual haunts. This species is found from the Ganges delta in India throughout South-east Asia and to as far as northern Australia.

The Saltwater crocodile is also the largest living species, some specimens reaching 20ft in length. One skull, owned by an Indian rajah, probably came from a crocodile 24½ft long.

▲A baby Australian freshwater crocodile breaks out of its eggshell.

▼A female Saltwater crocodile sits on guard on top of the huge nest mound in which she has laid her eggs.

Other large crocodiles include the American crocodile at 23ft, the Nile crocodile at 22ft, and the gharial at 21ft. Nowadays it is difficult to find a crocodile of anything like this size.

LAST OF THE LINE

Crocodiles are an ancient group. They lived alongside the dinosaurs and have changed little in the last 65 million years. But for some species, the chances of surviving for even another 10 or 20 years are poor. Even as recently as 1950, there were large numbers of crocodiles in some parts of the world. But in the 1950s and 60s a demand for crocodile skins for leather bags and shoes led to the deaths of untold numbers of crocodiles.

All species are now on the danger list. Large crocodiles were killed first. Mothers guarding nests made easy targets. Then hunters moved on to smaller specimens. Young animals were not allowed to grow old enough to breed and, with the breeding animals gone, numbers plummeted.

Although crocodiles produce large clutches of eggs, many eggs and young are taken by predators, floods and other hazards. Even in good conditions, only a tiny percentage of young survives. Most crocodiles take several years to grow into adults. The Saltwater crocodile, for example, may be 10 years old before it breeds for the first time. All species need help if they are to survive.

USEFUL CROCS

It may seem unimportant that a big, sometimes dangerous, animal such as a crocodile does survive. But crocodiles form a vital part of the balance of nature. In some lakes in Africa where crocodiles have disappeared, fishermen have suffered. The crocodiles ate large fish which fed on the small fish that the fishermen were catching. With the crocodiles gone, more large fish survived and ate more of the small fish.

CROCODILE CONSERVATION

The gharial was nearly hunted to extinction. In 1974, fewer than 60 adults survived in India. But now, large sanctuaries have been created. Eggs are collected and then incubated artificially so more baby gharials will hatch out. Babies are reared until they are about 4ft long. Then they can be released into the wild. Several thousand gharials now live in sanctuaries, but until they are breeding well we cannot say they are safe. In some places, the mugger and other crocodiles have similar protection.

▼Crocodiles often wait at water holes to ambush their prey. This Nile crocodile has caught an impala.

GLOSSARY

Adaptation Any feature of an animal that fits it to live in its surroundings. It can be something about the way the animal is built – such as the webbed feet of a turtle – or it can be something it does.

Adult A fully developed animal that is mature and capable of breeding.

Alpine Belonging to the Alps or any other high mountains. Usually used for heights that are over 5,000ft.

Amphibian An animal of the Class Amphibia. Members of this class generally have a larval stage dependent on water and an adult stage that lives on land, and smooth scale-less skins.

Amphibious Capable of living both in water and on land.

Aquatic Living in or near the water.

Arboreal Living in trees.

Bask To hold the body in a position directly exposed to the Sun.

Body temperature The temperature of the interior of an animal's body.

Brood The group of young raised in a single breeding cycle.

Brood pouch A special space in which young are kept during development.

Browse To feed on shoots, leaves and bark of shrubs and trees.

Cloaca In reptiles and amphibians, the chamber, opening to the outside of the body, into which discharge both liquid and solid waste, and also eggs and sperm during reproduction.

Cloud forest Damp forest, usually high on mountains, with dense undergrowth, ferns and mosses, and orchids growing on the trees.

Clutch The group of eggs laid by a female at a single laying.

Cocoon A protective covering for an animal's eggs or sub-adult stage.

Colonize To invade a new area and establish a breeding group.

Constriction A method of killing prey used by some snakes. The body is coiled tightly round the prey, suffocating it.

Courtship The period when an animal tries to attract a mate or renews its bonds with a mate from previous years.

Crest A raised structure running along the back of the body or head.

Crustaceans Members of the group of jointed-legged animals that includes shrimps, crabs, woodlice and waterfleas.

Direct development In amphibians, changing from egg to adult without going through a larval stage.

Display A pattern of things done by one animal that gives information to other animals. It may be seen or heard. Greeting, courtship or threatening may involve displays between animals.

Distribution The area in the world in which a species is found.

Eft A young newt that is beginning its life on land.

Egg-tooth A small tooth at the front of the upper jaw which helps a reptile or bird cut its way out of its egg at hatching. The egg-tooth is then lost.

Embryo A young amphibian or reptile developing within its egg.

Environment The surroundings of a particular species, or the world about us in general.

External fertilization Joining of eggs and sperm outside the female's body.

Family In classification of animals, a group of Species which share many features in common and are thought to be related, such as all the cobras.

Frog A tail-less amphibian with smooth skin.

Gill A structure in water-living animals through which exchange of oxygen and carbon dioxide takes place. For example, the feathery gills behind the head of frog tadpoles.

Glands Organs that produce a special chemical (secretion) that may be passed (secreted) to the outside world.

Habitat The surroundings in which an animal lives, including the plant life, other animals, physical surroundings and climate.

Hatchling An animal just emerged from its egg.

Hibernation A winter period in which an animal is inactive. In hibernation the body processes, such as beating of the heart, slow down as the body temperature falls.

Home range The area in which an individual animal normally lives.

Incubation Keeping eggs warm so that development can take place.

Internal fertilization Joining of eggs and sperm inside a female's body.

Introduced Describes an animal that has been brought by humans to a particular area where it previously did not occur. Introduction may be deliberate or accidental.

Invertebrate Any animal without a backbone e.g. insects, worms, crabs and slugs.

Juvenile A young animal that is no longer a baby, but is not yet fully adult.

Larva An early stage in the life-cycle of an animal such as an amphibian after it hatches from the egg. Usually it has a very different form from the adult, for example a frog tadpole.

Mammal Animals whose females have mammary glands, which produce milk on which they feed their young.

Marine Living in the sea.

Metamorphosis A change in structure of an animal as it goes from one stage of its life history to the next, as when a tadpole changes to a frog or any larva changes to an adult.

Migration The long distance movement of animals. It is typically seasonal and for the purpose of feeding or breeding.

Mucus A sticky, slimy substance produced by some membranes, such as many amphibian skins.

Newt Name given to some salamanders, especially those with amphibious habits.

Nocturnal Active during the night.

Omnivorous An animal that has a varied diet, eating both plants and animals.

Opposable Can be put opposite one another. Our thumb is opposable to our fingers.

Order The division of animal classification below Class and above Family. For example, all the frog and toad families belong in the order Anura.

Pigment A substance that gives color to an animal's body.

Pit receptor A hole (pit) containing cells sensitive to heat, found on the side of the head, or along the lips, in some groups of snake.

Placenta A structure attached to the inside of the female's reproductive system through which an embryo gets nourishment.

Plastron The part of a turtle's shell across the belly.

Population A separate group of animals of the same species.

Prairie A type of open grassland found in North America.

Predator An animal that hunts and kills other animals, its prey.

Prehensile Able to grasp, as the tail of a chameleon.

Rain forest A type of forest found in the tropics and sub-tropics that has a heavy rainfall throughout the year. Such forests usually contain a large number of different species. Some rain forest occurs in temperate regions, as in the Pacific north-west of the USA.

Salamander A type of tailed amphibian.

Savannah Tropical grassland, particularly in Africa.

Scent gland Special organs or areas of skin that produce chemicals that have a distinctive smell. The scent may not be detectable by humans. Scents are an important means of communication in some reptiles and amphibians.

Scrub A type of vegetation in which shrubs are the main part. It occurs naturally in some dry areas, or can be produced by human destruction of forest.

Solitary Living alone, not in a group.

Species The division of animal classification below Genus; a group of animals of the same structure that can breed together.

Spermatophore A packet of sperm passed from male to female, as in many salamanders.

Tadpole Strictly, the larva of a frog or toad, but also sometimes used to refer to larval salamanders.

Terrestrial Living on land.

Territory The area in which an animal or group of animals lives and defends against intruders.

Toad Any stout-bodied, warty-skinned frog, especially a type living in damp conditions but away from water.

Tortoise A land-living shelled reptile.

Turtle A water-living shelled reptile. In Europe, the term turtle is most often used when referring to sea-living species, the freshwater species being called terrapins.

Vertebrate Animals with backbones. All amphibians and reptiles are vertebrates.

INDEX

Scientific names

The first name of each double-barrel Latin name refers to the *Genus*, the second to the *species*. Single names not in *italic* refer to a family or sub-family and are cross-referenced to the Common name index.

FURTHER READING

Alexander, R. McNeill (ed) (1986), *The Encyclopedia of Animal Biology,* Facts On File, New York.

Berry, R.J. and Hallam, A. (eds) (1986), *The Encyclopedia of Animal Evolution*, Facts On File, New York.

Bellairs, A.d'A. and Cox, C.B. (eds) (1976), *Morphology and Biology of Reptiles*, Academic Press, London.

Carr, A. (1963), *The Reptiles*, Life Nature Library, New York.

Cochran, D.M. (1961), *Living Amphibians of the World*, Doubleday and Co., Garden City, New York.

Englemann, W.-E. and Obst, F.J. (1981), *Snakes. Biology, Behavior and Relationships to Man*, Edition Leipzig, Leipzig.

Ferguson, M.W.J. (ed) (1984), *The Structure, Development and Evolution of Reptiles*, Academic Press, London.

Goin, C.J., Goin, O.B. and Zug, G.R. (1978), *Introduction to Herpetology* (3rd edition), W.H.Freeman and Co., San Francisco.

Halliday, T.R. and Adler, K. (eds) (1985), *The Enyclopedia of Reptiles and Amphibians*, Facts On File, New York.

Moore, P.D. (ed) (1986), *The Encyclopedia of Animal Ecology*, Facts On File, New York.

Parker, H.W. and Grandison, A.G.C. (1977), *Snakes, a Natural History*, British Museum (Nat Hist), London, and Cornell University Press, Ithaca, New York.

Peters, J.A. (1964), *Dictionary of Herpetology*, Hafner Publishing Co, New York.

Porter, K.R. (1972), *Herpetology*, W.B. Saunders Co, Philadelphia.

Russell, F.E. (1980), *Snake Venom Poisoning*, J.B.Lippincott Co, Philadelphia.

Slater, P.J.B. (ed) (1986), *The Encyclopedia of Animal Behavior*, Facts On File, New York.

ACKNOWLEDGMENTS

Picture credits

Key: *t* top. *b* bottom. *c* center. *l* left. *r* right.
Abbreviations: A Ardea. AN Agence Nature. ANT Australasian Nature Transparencies. BCL Bruce Coleman Ltd. CAH C.A. Henley. DMD David M. Dennis. FL Frank Lane Agency. MF Michael Fogden. NHPA Natural History Photographic Agency. NSP Natural Science Photos. OSF Oxford Scientific Films. P Premaphotos Wildlife/K. Preston Mafham. PEP Planet Earth Pictures/Seaphot. RWVD R.W. van Devender. SAL Survival Anglia Ltd.

8*t* Nature Photographers/S. Bisserot. 8*b* NHPA. 10 NHPA/ Jany Sauvanet. 11*t* MF. 11*b* RWVD. 12 OSF/G. Bernard. 13, 14 DMD. 15 NHPA/R.J. Erusin. 18-19, 20-21 BCL/Jack Dermid. 21 OSF/J. Dermid. 22-23 Nature Photographers. 23 MF. 26 NSP/C. Mattison. 26-27 MF. 28-29 NHPA/S. Dalton. 30 MF. 31*t* DMD. 31*c* MF. 35 NHPA. 36 PEP/C. Pétron. 37 Dr H.R. Bustard. 41 A/F. Gohier. 42 Biofotos/Heather Angel. 43 Nature Photographers/S. Bisserot. 44-45 OSF. 47 MF. 49*t* G. Mazza. 49*b* NHPA/H. Switak. 50-51 BCL. 51 P. 52-53 A/H. Dossenbach. 54 MF. 55*l* NSP/C. Mattison. 55*r* CAH. 56 G. Mazza. 57 Frithfoto. 59*t* Biofotos/S. Summerhays. 59*b* A/H. & J. Beste. 62*tl*, 62*b* MD. 65*t* Frithfoto. 65*b* BCL/G. Zeisler. 67 SAL/Alan Root. 69*t* A. Bannister. 69*b* NSP/C. Banks. 70 A. Bannister. 71 NHPA/A. Bannister. 72-73 BCL/Allan Power. 74 NHPA/J. Shaw. 75*t* MF. 75*b* RWVD. 76 A. Bannister. 76-77 NHPA/S. Dalton. 78 RWVD. 79 G. Mazza. 80, 81, 82 Biofotos/Heather Angel. 83 BCL/Jane Burton. 84-85 AN/Lanceau. 88*t* NSP/C. Banks. 88*b* ANT/D.B. Carter. 89 SAL/A. Root.

Artwork credits.

Abbreviations: DD David Dennis. DO Denys Ovenden. HAG Hayward Art Group. RL Richard Lewington. SD Simon Driver.

6, 7*t*, 7*bl* SD. 7*br*, 9 HAG. 13 DO. 14-15, 16 DD. 16*cl* DO. 16*b*, 20-21, 24-25 DD. 28 DO. 29, 30 DD. 32, 32-33, 33, 34*t* HAG. 34*b*, 35 SD. 37 DD. 38 DO. 39, 40, 43, 46, 47, 48-49 DD. 53 DO. 55 DD. 58*t* DO. 58*b*, 60-61, 62-63, 64 DD. 65 SD. 68 DO. 70 SD. 73 RL. 83, 86-87 DD.